7 ESSENTIALS TO *grow your Marriage*

by

Steve & Cindy Wright

PUBLISHED BY PREVAIL PRESS

7 ESSENTIALS TO grow your Marriage

by

Steve & Cindy Wright

Copyright © 2018 by Steve and Cindy Wright

Book Design by Robert Swanson

Published by Prevail Press

All rights reserved. No part of this book may be reproduced or transmitted in any form or by any means, electronic or mechanical, including photocopying, recording, or by any information storage and retrieval system, without permission in writing from the publisher.

ISBN-13:

978-1-948824-00-2 Paperback

978-1-948824-90-3 e-Book

Attributions

NIV

Scripture quotations marked NIV are taken from the Holy Bible, New International Version®, NIV®. Copyright © 1973, 1978, 1984, 2011 by Biblica, Inc.™ Used by permission of Zondervan.

All rights reserved worldwide.

www.zondervan.com the "NIV" and "New International Version" are trademarks registered in the United States Patent and Trademark Office by Biblica, Inc.™

ESV

Scripture quotations marked ESV are from The ESV® Bible (The Holy Bible, English Standard Version®), copyright © 2001 by Crossway, a publishing ministry of Good News Publishers. Used by permission.

All rights reserved.

The Message

Scripture quotations marked MSG are taken from THE MESSAGE, copyright © 1993, 1994, 1995, 1996, 2000, 2001, 2002 by Eugene H. Peterson. Used by permission of NavPress.

All rights reserved. Represented by Tyndale House Publishers, Inc.

Dedication

This is a very hard thing for us to do because there are hundreds of people who have been influential in our lives, marriage and ministry over the years. And if we started to name them we would be afraid that we would leave someone's name off an important list like this. Just know that if you have touched our lives in any way, we love and appreciate you.

But there is one couple in particular that we do want to dedicate this book to. They have been mentors, ministry partners and most importantly, friends, for more than 30 years. They counseled and challenged us through the lean years of starting up Marriage Missions International. They believed in us and wouldn't let us give up. We believe it's safe to say without their involvement and influence in our lives Marriage Missions wouldn't be where it is today; nor would we ever have been able to write this book.

Through their lives and marriage they have exemplified each of the seven essentials we will share with you. To our very dear friends, Steve and Mary Marr, thanks for pouring your wisdom and love into us all these years. You are friends forever!

> "And friends are friends forever If the Lord's the Lord of them. And a friend will not say never 'Cause the welcome will not end. In the Father's hands we know that a lifetime's not too long to live as friends."
>
> Michael W. Smith
From the song, *Friends*

7 Essentials to Growing Your Marriage

FORWARD

by
Eric & Jennifer Garcia

They are real people, with a real marriage, and a real journey. Steve and Cindy are giving all of us a gift. This gift is a front row seat to their struggles and determination to see God grow their marriage. This level of transparency is where life change begins. Their journey is expressed through their 7 Essentials. The very life essentials that helped them grow is now available to all of us. This is a powerful message from a couple that is committed to their marriage, even through the challenges. We have served in ministry with Steve and Cindy, and are excited to see their hearts expressed in a practical way to help others grow their marriages.

Eric & Jennifer Garcia

Co-founders, Association of Marriage and Family Ministries (AMFM)

Table of Contents

Forward..7

Introduction...11

Marriage Essential #1
Build a Solid Foundation for Your Marriage:
Committed to God and to Each Other..13

Marriage Essential #2
Be Intentional In Growing Your Love Relationship............................41

Marriage Essential #3
Renvigorating Your Romance and Sex Life...67

Marriage Essential #4
Guard Your Heart, Mind, and Your Marriage......................................101

Marriage Essential #5
Fight the Good Fight: Resolve Conflict in Healthy Ways..................131

Marriage Essential #6
Stand United: Don't Let Family, Friends, or Things Separate You...157

Marriage Essential #7
Partner with God and Each Otherto Make an Impact on Your World.187

INTRODUCTION

In our ministry, we hear every week from people who say, "God wants me to be happy!" or "God doesn't want me to be unhappy." This phrase is linked to their explanation as to why they are divorcing their spouse. To that Cindy and I say, "Horse Hockey!" We often write back to the person who says this and ask them to show us in the Bible where it says God wants them to be happy. So far, we've never gotten a response back. It's just not there.

Now, we will also admit that God does not want anyone to be miserable in his or her marriage either. True, the Bible says "But those who marry will face many troubles in this life" (1 Corinthians 7:28). But that does not mean we have to be miserable; misery is optional. And so is joy in married life.

Cindy and I have been in both camps over our 46+ years of marriage... early on there was more misery. But when we began to work together to make our marriage great we have had more joy-filled days and experiences (even in troubling times), than we could have ever imagined in the early days.

In the following pages, we have shared from our experiences and our hearts what we think are the ESSENTIALS for all married couples to experience the same kind of joy we have attained. We won't try to kid you – what you are about to read will require a commitment to God and each other to apply what you will learn. But we can promise you it will be worth it.

We thank you for taking this challenge and even though we may never know your names we will be praying that you will get EXACTLY what God wants you to take away from this book. After you are done we welcome your feedback. You can share with us at email@marriagemissions.com.

MARRIAGE ESSENTIAL #1
BUILD A SOLID FOUNDATION FOR YOUR MARRIAGE:
COMMITTED TO GOD AND TO EACH OTHER

If you are contemplating marriage, or if you are newly married, GREAT! You are in the "wet cement" time of your budding relationship. It's like what Robert Wolgemuth says, "The first year of marriage is like wet cement—the impressions made in it are much harder to change once it has set." This is a time when you can start to build a solid foundation without having to bust up those hardened habits you already have established. It's a lot easier to start out fresh in building a solid, healthy, loving foundation than it is to tear one down and start again. It is our prayer that as you begin reading, you can glean solid principles that you can then apply to your lives together.

If you've been married for a while—perhaps even decades—that's good too. As you read on, you may discover that you have already built a solid foundation for your marriage. If so that is wonderful. It's still possible though, that you can learn a few additional pointers you haven't thought of before that will only strengthen your marriage even more.

If your marriage finds itself on shaky ground at this time in your life, please view the title of this chapter as if it reads: "REBUILD or BUILD FOR THE FIRST TIME... a Solid Foundation for Your Marriage." Yes, rebuilding is more difficult than building for the first time. You may need to tear down the shaky foundation (old habits and hardened ways of doing things) that has previously been set in place. But then you can build a new foundation that truly is solid, which will prevent you from running into damaging relational situations in the future. We're talking about a foundation that can hold you both up in your marriage. No matter what you may have faced, or are dealing with now, this is not an impossible task.

Our prompting would be to start anew. Each day can be a new beginning. Just because you've been married for a while, it doesn't mean that you can't commit to rebuilding your marriage foundation so it is as solid as it is possible "from this day forward." Put your hand into God's and into your spouse's and commit to it. It is so worth it! We know from firsthand experience. We had to do this in our own marriage. And we are here to tell you that it is possible. If we can do it, anyone can.

Sometimes in marriage, it's important to learn new things to accomplish that, which is before you. Other times it's necessary to unlearn some things that have caused problems. Whether you're in the "Wet Cement" years where bad habits haven't set in so deeply yet, or you're in a more hardened place, it's important to get it right. Make it right, if you need to. It may be difficult to do what is needed to build and secure the foundation of your marriage. But once you put into place a solid foundation, storms can hit you (which they will), but you will stand together strong.

Be wise and build your home—your marriage—upon the Solid Rock of Jesus Christ. Remember Jesus' words as recorded in Matthew 7:24-27. He said:

> "Everyone then who hears these words of mine and does them will be like a wise man who built his house on the rock. And the rain fell, and the floods came, and the winds blew and beat on that house, but it did not fall, because it had been founded on the rock. And everyone who hears these words of mine and does not do them will be like a foolish man who built his house on the sand. And the rain fell, and the floods came, and the winds blew and beat against that house, and it fell, and great was the fall of it."
>
> - NLT

These are important words to remember as you build your marriage, or rebuild it.

Once again, the marriage essential we gave is:

"Build a solid foundation for your marriage: committed to God and to each other."

Because a marriage is built by combining masculine and feminine viewpoints, we offer both, through Cindy's perspective and Steve's.

Cindy

In that scripture passage, we're told to build our house upon the rock, instead of sand. The question is, can your marital house still stand if it is presently built on a less than solid foundation? Yes, under "normal" conditions many houses, even if they are built on a shaky foundation, can still stand. We've seen this happen. But Jesus gives this warning for a reason. Woe the house that comes up against a whopper storm. I believe Jesus gives this warning because of those storms. He's telling us that they're coming. We can't say that we haven't been warned, especially given the circumstances of the world in which we live.

We are told in the Bible that God "sends rain on the just and on the unjust (NKJV)." That means that everyone is subject to storms that will, at one time or another, hit against our houses—our marriages. I don't know of any marriage that escapes them. In 1 Corinthians 7:28, the apostle Paul writes that "those who marry will face many troubles in this life (NIV)." Anyone who has been married more than a few days can attest to the fact that we all face troubled times in our marriages. Storms hit us all—some caused by outside forces and others caused from within.

Our Storm

That's precisely what happened to us. Our marriage was sailing along smoothly. Like any normal couple, we had the usual spats here and there over issues. However, when Steve became sick and went to the doctor, little did we know that his diagnosis would change our life. It also changed the whole tone of our marriage from that point onward. After what we thought would be a routine doctor's appointment, Steve came home and told me that he had been diagnosed with diabetes. And what's especially scary about it was that it was Type 1 Diabetes. That's the type that brings the serious health problems and other complications with it.

Usually, a patient is placed on an insulin regimen immediately. because a Type 1 diabetic's body no longer is capable of producing insulin. Your body needs insulin to adequately process the sugars you ingest, or you will die.

Unfortunately, Steve's doctor didn't know a lot about Diabetes control. When Steve refused to take shots, he had Steve try the pills that Type 2 Diabetics use to stimulate their pancreas into working. That was a mistake. There was no stimulating Steve's pancreas; it appeared to have totally given up. We found out later that Steve had a virus when he wasn't feeling well and it took down his pancreas at that time.

Two Major Problems (Among Many)

There were two problems (among many) that this caused. First, it changed Steve's personality. He was no longer the happy-go-lucky guy he was before. He became moody and didn't feel good most of the time. Part of this was due to the fact that he needed insulin, not pills, as part of his regimen. Steve was not a "good" diabetic and didn't take good care of his health, which is vital in working with this disease. He became moody and soon became very disagreeable to live with.

Secondly, I was in total shock. The dad of one of my best friends, when I was a teenager, was a diabetic. He eventually became bedridden, went blind, and died after suffering for several miserable years. I swore I would never marry a diabetic. Now, several years later, I found myself married to one. Fear gripped my heart because of those painful past memories. Was this going to be my future—being married to a sickly, dying man?

What added to the shock, and my fear was the fact that Steve wasn't taking good care of his diabetes. (My friend's father didn't either.) As a result, Steve and I argued a lot about this, and a whole lot more. Sadly, I wasn't exactly Mrs. Maturity, who could handle this very well (although I thought I was). So we had major problems going on in our relationship.

Remember the scripture that talked about the house falling that was built upon the sand (shaky ground)? "The winds blew and beat against that house, and it fell. And great was that fall." That was happening to us. The winds of adversity blew and beat us up emotionally pretty badly. We weren't prepared for the adversity that had blindsided us, and as a result, our house proceeded to crumble. Eventually, I left Steve with our young son, and had every intention of divorcing him. But God...

I say, "but God" as a dramatic pause, because it was. Someone once said, "Practice the pause. When in doubt, pause. When angry, pause, When tired, pause. When stressed, pause. And when you pause, pray." Well, I didn't know how to pray very well. I paused, but not very long. I didn't believe much in God at that time. I was ready to take action in getting out of what I considered to be a loveless marriage. I thought that once you "fell" out of love that you could never get it back again. I was wrong, but I didn't know it at the time.

Light Shining Through the Darkness

It was at this time that my best friend Jessie had just given her life to Jesus, asking Him to come into her life and be her Lord and Savior. She became a totally changed person. I didn't know this at the time until I saw her. When she found out I was in town (I went to my parents' house out of town), she met with me and talked to me about the Lord and the new changes that were taking place in her life. I definitely saw those changes. God stirred deeply within my heart, so I also asked the Jesus to be the Savior of my life. All of a sudden, when my life looked so dark and bleak, as far as my future, I saw a glimmer of light and hope.

The first thing Jessie told me (as God led her) was: "Go back home to Steve. Put everything on pause again. Don't worry about Steve; God will talk to him." She also told me to read the Bible as if it was real (I didn't believe it was at the time).

I questioned Jessie about this. I said, "But Steve is the same person I left. He hasn't changed at all. Why should I do this?" Jessie told me, through God's leading, to watch to see what God would do. That is because from this day forth, I would never be the same, and neither would be the journey of my life. And she (God within her) was right.

What's "funny" about all of this is that I was usually a skeptical person. I tend to want things to be proven to me before I'll do anything about it. But when God stirred within my heart, He also gave me a huge dose of peace about all the hardships I was facing. I did what I was told all by blind faith. That truly was a miracle! I still stand amazed by all of this.

Change and a New Hope

Within two weeks, Steve sat me down and asked me what had happened to me. He saw a change, and he liked it. Honestly, I hadn't even noticed I had changed. I told him about my asking Christ to be my Savior. I told him about the divorce I was planning (which he was unaware of until then... he just knew things were serious). And I told him about reading the Bible Jessie had given me. For some reason it was making sense, which I now know was all God's doing. God's presence in my life was changing my whole outlook on everything. I felt hope, peace, and optimism towards life in a way I had never felt before.

At that point, God stirred within Steve's heart. He told me that he wanted what I had and prayed to receive Jesus as His personal Savior. We didn't totally make Jesus Lord of our lives until a while afterward. But we were on our way. And from that day forward, our life started to point in a more positive direction. It didn't all change at once. It was actually two steps forward and then one step back... sometimes it was even the reverse. But it was a good start. We were at least falling forward, rather than falling backward into a toxic relationship.

Now, let me say here that we realize that Steve's coming to faith so quickly is unusual. We see that the unbelieving spouse usually takes a lot longer to accept Jesus as Savior. But this is what happened with us. Even so, many times marriages turn around quickly in a positive direction once there is a positive spiritual change of heart. Ours didn't. I'm not sure why. It may be because of our stubbornness, immaturity, or a whole host of reasons. But we were at least pointed in the right direction, and God was definitely at work within both of us.

I've told you a bit about our story, hoping that those of you who find yourself at a shaky place in your marriage will feel a glimmer of hope. You can start building anew a solid foundation –one that can help you to build a GREAT marriage. There will be some changes that need to be made. But they are good changes that will transform your marriage. But it starts with a willing heart, and eventually two willing hearts.

Falling Forward in Marriage

I have to say at this point that even though we got our hearts in the right place, we had to get our minds and commitment lined up, as well. It was a slow, uphill battle for us, with lots of mistakes being made. But that's okay. It was worth it, even though I wondered sometimes.

We wish we had access to the information we now know, but we didn't. We had to learn the hard way, falling forward step-by-step. Eventually, we did get a hold of the info we needed. Much of it is now posted on the Marriage Missions website. And so you now have access to it as well. We believe it is our God-given mission to help others build good foundations for their marriage relationships.

Please take advantage of what we have posted, along with the other websites and resources we recommend. Why take the hard(er) route when you can go an easier one? I'm not saying it's an easy journey, but it's sure a lot easier than you might have had if you don't take advantage of that. There are many marriage "experts" and experienced spouses who can help teach you in the journey to wholeness. The info we are about to share with you can be of tremendous help, as it has and is helping us to build our home—our marriage—upon the solid rock of Jesus Christ and all He can teach us and empower us to do.

Marriages Centering on Christ

Frankly, I don't know how any marriage that is not built upon Jesus can stand. Many do. On the outside, many seem to. And surprisingly, there are some that appear to have quite good marriages without Christ. But I don't believe they could ever be. Without God in the center of it, they are missing out on His many blessings and eternal purpose for their lives. They may be good, yes, by the world's standards, but not good by God's standards. There is more to marriage than simply a husband and wife centered on their own happiness, or their children's. God has an eternal purpose and plan for couples. And yes, I do believe there is usually a lot of happiness involved. Yet that is not the main goal. It is a goal to look to, as God leads. Loving God, loving each other, as God would have us, loving others and pointing them to Christ, are actually the goals I believe God would have us embrace.

What's especially sad, though, is that there are many so-called "Christian" marriages that don't reflect the love or the ways of Christ. This should not be so! Christians should have the BEST marriages ever! As Christ followers, we personally know the living God, whose very name means love. Who is better at teaching us how to love and live with each other than our God of love? No one. The problem is that many of us don't listen, follow, and apply what He has for us to learn. If we did... Wow! We would see the most amazing marriages happening all over the world. It would be miraculous. And it still can be, because God is not dead, and neither are we.

So, my first piece of advice, pertaining to the marriage essential is to "build a solid foundation for your marriage—committed to God and to each other." Here are a few additional commitments I believe are essential in building that solid foundation:

TOTALLY commit your life to Jesus Christ, to be your Savior and your Lord

Don't worry about your spouse—you stand alone before the Lord on this one. Commit your life to the Lord, asking Him to lead you every day in small and large ways. Even if your spouse never commits his or her life in this way to Jesus, be wise. Your eternal destiny and the direction of your life depend upon this. Don't waver in your commitment to the Lord. Commit yourself wholeheartedly to God and He will guide you through good times and tough ones, as you lean upon Him.

As God tugs on your heart, commit it all to Him. Tell Him everything you can think of that you have done wrong. Don't talk to Him at this time about the things your spouse has done. That is between your spouse and God. This time of inner reflection is between you and God. Talk to Him as your Heavenly Father (because He is). Tell Him what you have done wrong and give it to Him.

We're told in the Bible, "If we confess our sins, He is faithful and just and will forgive us our sins and purify us from all unrighteousness" (1 John 1:9 NIV). In other words, no matter what we have done that is wrong, if we confess it all to the Lord, and we're truly sorry for the wrongs we have done, God will forgive us and will not hold any of it against us.

Ask Jesus to come into your life in a personal way and commit, from this day forward, to do things His way. If you do, you will start a spiritual journey that will change your life forever, as the Lord has changed us, our individual lives, and married life together. If you haven't already done this, I pray you will take this step right now. (And if you want to know more about this spiritual journey, please contact us through the Marriage Missions International website.)

Then talk to God about your spouse and the concerns you have. Ask God to show you what to do about "our" marital concerns.

Put it all out there for Him and then join spiritual hands with Him to walk in His way, rather than what seems to make sense to you. God tells us in Isaiah 55:9, "For my thoughts are not your thoughts, neither are your ways my ways," declares the Lord. "As the heavens are higher than the earth, so are my ways higher than your ways and my thoughts than your thoughts."

God sees everything from a higher and wiser perspective than we can see them. What makes sense to Him is what truly will make a difference.

Go a step further. Commit to Jesus, and commit to follow what we're told in the Bible

Don't just be a "Bible-believing follower of Jesus, be a Bible-*living* follower. These are two separate steps. You must believe with your mind and heart, but you also must believe with your actions. Too many people forget that obedience is the true demonstration of faith. They fail to connect the dots. Words without actions are empty.

We're told in God's word:

> "Do not merely listen to the word, and so deceive yourselves. Do what it says. Anyone who listens to the word but does not do what it says is like someone who looks at his face in a mirror and, after looking at himself, goes away and immediately forgets what he looks like. But whoever looks intently into the perfect law that gives freedom, and continues in it—not forgetting what they have heard, but doing it —they will be blessed in what they do. Those who consider themselves

religious and yet do not keep a tight rein on their tongues deceive themselves, and their religion is worthless."

- James 1:22-26
NIV

We are to be "doers, not merely hearers only." It's important to live what we say we believe. Do you call yourself a Christian—a follower of Jesus Christ? Then whatever you are faced with in your marriage, always consider, "What would Jesus do?" In other words, "What would Jesus have ME do?" If you leave Him out, you put your feet and marriage upon shaky ground.

Read your Bible and then go and APPLY what you learn to your own life and your relationship with your spouse. Those aren't empty words or suggestions. God wouldn't have it written out in the Bible and in your heart if He didn't mean for you to apply what He told us to do. The principles for loving your spouse are the principles for living, which we can read about throughout the Bible. Read and apply all of God's wisdom, no matter how hard it is. That is God's will for you.

Commit to showing love to your spouse, as you promised you would in your wedding vows

Wedding vows are sacred words. You are making a covenant promise when you say your vow to your future spouse. You are making promises to your spouse, but you are also making promises before God and to God, in the presence of "many witnesses"—all those you invited to your wedding. That is a part of the reason why God takes our stated wedding vows very seriously. And so should we. If we don't consider these vows as a serious commitment "until we are parted by death" as we promised, then we shouldn't say them. We should just stay single. No one is making you state these promises. It is your choice to enter into a covenant relationship with another.

Another reason God takes our wedding vows seriously is because marriage is a type of living picture of Christ's love for the church (those who claim to know Him in a committed way). In this picture, Jesus is the Bridegroom, and His church is His Bride. The couple that is marrying is committing themselves to live out this picture in their everyday lives together.

We live in a world where we're with many skeptical people who are watching the way we treat each other in our married life. They are watching because those who claim to be followers of Jesus Christ are seen as His representatives. These people long to see the pure, faithful love of God authentically lived out. So take this a step further. When we hurt each other, and we break our vows, what do these actions say to those who don't know the Lord in a personal way? Think about the message they could pick up about the faithful commitment the Lord has for His Bride, and the faithful commitment the Bride has for her Bridegroom?

Again, I ask the question, are you a follower of Jesus Christ? If your answer is yes—my next question is, are you a Bible-believing, Bible-LIVING Christian? If you aren't, then you are building the foundation of your marital relationship on shaky ground, as if it were placed upon shifting sand. What you believe and the way you live will have more of a tendency to shift around. You will embrace what sounds good to you, rather than what the Word of God says is good.

If you said yes, that you are a Bible-living Christian, then show your spouse Christ-like love. Don't give it according to the way he or she shows you love, but give the type of love that Jesus has given to you. In John 13:34-35, ESV it is recorded that Jesus said:

> "A new commandment I give to you, that you love one another: just as I have loved you, you also are to love one another. By this all people will know that you are my disciples, if you have love for one another."

Author Gary Thomas gives the following challenge in support of these words of Jesus:

> "If somebody tried to describe your love for God solely by how well you show love to your spouse, what would they say?"

Hopefully, they will say that the way you interact with your spouse reveals and reflects the love of Christ, from the inside out. As a result, God is lifted up, and He is able to use your good testimony to draw others to Himself.

Lastly, commit to your marriage. Grow to be the spouse God would have you be

When you marry, you go from being single-focused, where you are primarily focused on your own needs, to marry your life and focus with one another. It's a lot like something Mike Mason wrote:

> "A marriage is not a joining of two worlds, but an abandoning of two worlds in order that one new one might be formed. In this sense, the call to be married bears comparison with Jesus' advice to the rich young man, which is to sell all his possessions and follow Him. It is a vocation to total abandonment. For most people, in fact, marriage is the single most wholehearted step they will ever take toward a fulfillment of Jesus' command to love one's neighbor as oneself."
>
> - Mike Mason
> "The Mystery of Marriage"

Marriage is an intertwining of two hearts and two lives to help each other live up to our God-designed full potential. Commit to the sacredness of this marital union. Commit to live up to the promises you made. Keep in mind:

> "God is the witness of every marriage ceremony, and will be the witness to every violation of its vows."
>
> - Thomas V. Moore

STEVE

Cindy already gave you the crux of our early years and what happened, but now I'd like to add some things that I saw as well… because we both saw the same things, but through different eyes and experiences.

Let me start by saying that when Cindy and I got married more than forty-six years ago, we had no clue what a good foundation for a marriage was—or why it was so important. Looking back, we didn't really know what love was. To us it was all based on feelings and what we could get out of the relationship more than what we could give to it. Oh, we had the normal arguments over issues like money, household chores, and the like, but nothing big happened that shook our world to really "test" our love and commitment to each other—until…

Just seven months into our "honeymoon" Cindy became pregnant. It wasn't completely unplanned because her doctor had told her she had a condition that could eventually prevent her from getting pregnant. His recommendation was to try to get pregnant as soon as possible, which we did (we were good at it). So, in July 1973 our first son, David, was born. This changed our lives dramatically—especially because he had colic the first three months of his life.

This meant that he cried a lot from constant intestinal distress, and there was nothing that could be done for it. His pediatrician said he would just "outgrow it." But a baby that cries constantly every evening for three months can add significant stress to your marriage. He's now in his 40s, and yes, he did outgrow it.

As Cindy shared before, in April 1974, when I was twenty-three, I was diagnosed as a Type-1/Juvenile Onset diabetic, which meant I would be on insulin the rest of my life. In 1974 much of the medical community and my doctor were still in the "dark ages" as far as really knowing how to best treat my diabetes. The prognosis for me to have a very long life appeared to be pretty dim at that time. I was pretty much on my own with little information to help me know how to manage my disease.

What made matters worse was that I rebelled at this news and did little to take care of myself. I became angry, belligerent, and, overall, not a nice person to be around. Unfortunately, Cindy got the worst of it. To be frank, I was a real jerk in how I treated her and others!

Though my diabetes was the absolute worst thing we could think of that could happen to us, it also became the "best thing," because this is what God used to bring us to Himself, as Cindy shared in her story.

God Opened My Eyes

When Cindy arrived home after a time of our being separated, I had no clue as to what happened to her while she was gone. However, when she walked through the door, I immediately could tell something was different about her. Her countenance had changed. She seemed to be more at peace... and happy. She didn't say a word to me about her newfound faith, but she lived her life differently each day. She was kinder in the way she treated me, and yet, I hadn't changed. I tell people that I was "slow, but not stupid." After about two weeks I sat her down and asked her what changed?

She shared with me everything that had recently transpired. She explained how she had embraced Jesus as her personal Savior. She felt new from the inside out. At that moment, it was as though the Holy Spirit removed the blinders from my eyes. That night I prayed to ask Christ to come into my life and change me, too. That was the start of building a new foundation for our lives and our marriage.

I'd *like* to say that God healed me of my diabetes, and life was fabulous from that day forward. That's what I'd like to say. But it would be a lie. I still had the same problems with my crummy attitude, and my health continued to be a problem. We still had the financial struggles young families have, and we still argued a lot.

Despite the challenges we still faced, we also had a common faith, and a desire to please God. Then the Lord blessed us with our first miracle since surrendering our lives to Him—Cindy became pregnant with our second son, John.

The Key

Why did we tell you this story? It's because none of what we are about to share would have ever happened if Cindy and I hadn't surrendered our lives to Jesus Christ and asked Him to become the foundation for our lives. He chose two very imperfect people, who still struggled in many areas of our marriage, and moved us to be His servants to help marriages, especially ours, to become healthy, loving, and foundationally strong.

The KEY for us... and for everyone... is to say YES to God. Yes to his offer of salvation through Christ alone, and yes to letting Him guide our lives as couples through the truths of the Bible. Here are the foundational elements we have built our marriage on that have worked for many, many years for us:

As stated before—having a personal relationship with Jesus Christ as Lord and Savior of your life is where you and we all start. If you're still unclear as to why this is so important, talk with a pastor or go to www.needhim.com.

People often ask us, "How can we have a marriage like yours?" Well, that's why we have created this resource. We wanted to share with you 7 ESSENTIALS to Grow Your Marriage. It all starts with:

FOUR FOUNDATIONAL PILLARS

Any good builder will tell you that the foundation is THE most important part of any construction project. The better the foundation, the better the structure that sits on it. Cindy already shared the verses from Matthew 7. Jesus was a carpenter. He knew how important a good foundation was, so He was well qualified to offer this illustration for us.

The words Jesus was referring to from the Matthew 7 passage were His teachings in the Sermon on the Mount. They start in Matthew, chapter 5, and go through the end of chapter 7. Matthew spent 111 verses outlining some of the important building blocks Jesus gave for us to build our lives and marriages upon.

He starts with the Beatitudes (the "Blessed are the...") and then moves into concepts such as: how we are to be salt and light; how to handle anger, lust, divorce, retaliation, making oaths, loving our enemies, and people who persecute us, etc.

From there, He covers many other foundational elements and truths of our faith-walk with Him. You need to study these for yourself, but I want to share the Four Pillars that have been the most pivotal for Cindy's and my marriage (foundationally speaking). We believe they are essential for you, as well, as you build a solid marital foundation.

PILLAR 1 – PRAY FOR, AND WITH, EACH OTHER

> "To be a Christian without prayer is no more possible than to be alive without breathing."
>
> - Martin Luther

This first pillar, in our estimation, is the most important, because if you don't pray together consistently the other three pillars will be on shaky ground.

In Matthew 6:5-14 Jesus "models" for us how we should approach our prayer time. He is not saying that we need to repeat, verbatim, what we know to be the "Lord's Prayer." Rather, He's saying we should start your prayers by acknowledging and praising God for who He is. Then you invite Him to have His will be done in your lives as husband and wife. Next, thank Him for His provisions to meet the needs (both physical and spiritual) in your home. Ask for His forgiveness for any sins/wrongs you may have committed against each other. And pray for His covering over you throughout the day to protect you from temptation and evil influences. It's a great outline to use.

This is how Cindy and I began our ritual/tradition of praying together every morning before I would leave the house for work more than forty years ago. When we first started this, I had to leave the house a little after 3:00 a.m. to go to work. So, I would kneel next to Cindy while she was still in bed. We would then hold hands and pray for each other, our kids, and anything that was pressing in on us. Even in the dark of our bedroom, it felt as though we were in the presence of God as we prayed together. It set a great course for each of us for the rest of our day.

I would have to say that our prayer time is what held us together during the worst of times (yes, we had them) in our marriage. When we were mad, fed-up, and disgusted to the point that we didn't even want to be in the same room together, God would always remind us that our foundation was built on Him and His forgiveness for us. This would prompt us to resolve any differences between us and come back together, which we did.

Yes, praying together was intimidating in the beginning. It was awkward and uncomfortable to pray out loud. That's why you keep your prayers short and focused. Cindy and I do this, where I'm the one who leads in our morning prayer times. There have been times when I've asked Cindy to lead because I wasn't in a "good place" right then or wasn't feeling well. Plus, she knows she always has the freedom to lead out whenever she feels prompted. I can assure you I don't think my prayers are any better than hers. This is just the way we conduct our joint prayer times. But for you, it may be different. And that is great. The point is, just do it regularly!

Believe me when I say there is no one format to do this. You can stumble all over yourselves, slur your speech, and mispronounce words. It doesn't matter because you aren't praying to each other; you are praying to God. He doesn't expect perfection from us. He simply wants us to come before Him to ask Him to guide and help us through our day and marriage. He wants us to be ourselves and talk to Him as we would talk to our best friend if they were sitting there with us.

We also believe the best practice is for you to do this privately, if possible (away from other people, kids, family). This gives you the freedom to pray/speak to God honestly about any issues that you wouldn't necessarily want others to hear. This is your time together with your God. However, it is also good for your kids to hear and see you praying together at times.

Here are a few other suggestions that may help you get started:

- Before you start, talk with each other about your thoughts and feelings about prayer and praying together. Make sure that your spouse knows that you are a safe person to pray with—that you are not judging how either one of you prays. Talk about your and your spouse's fears in as open a way as possible. Talk also about your expectations up front, so they don't trip you up later on, as you pray with each other.

- Pick a time and commit to each other to begin praying together during that time you have now decided to set aside. It's hard to get started praying together regularly if you don't make a commitment to a specific, agreed-upon time. Cindy and I agreed that the best/easiest time for us to do this consistently was before I left for work every morning. For you, it may be before you turn off the lights when you're in bed.

- Don't be upset or feel condemned if you miss a day. It's important, however, if you miss a day, to start again the next day. Nobody's perfect and "the challenges of life" can happen. God is not waiting with a checklist, watching to see if you pray every day... and if you don't He'll send a plague upon you.

- First, start small and grow from there. Most anyone can put five or ten minutes into his or her life, as opposed to one hour. If you don't have that small amount of time, then you may need to do some rearranging of your schedule and priorities.

- Agree from the start that neither one of you will "sermonize" during your time of prayer. Nothing can stop the process like using the time to pray together as a way to preach to your spouse, or to make suggestions in your prayer.

I promise you (from personal experience) the more you do this together the easier it becomes. In fact, it will get to the place where the first thing you'll want to do when something difficult comes up in your lives is to pray together.

Let me add one more thought on this Pillar, just for the husbands. I can't stress how important it is for us to also cover our wives with prayer every day. And if you're wondering, "How can I do that?" I have a page of prayer points I've posted on our website that you can download and use as a way to get started.

Here's the link:

https://marriagemissions.com/praying-wife-head-toe

And here's a link for wives:

https://marriagemissions.com/prayer-husband-head-toe

We're also putting together some additional Prayer Pages for husbands and wives... so keep an eye out for that to be available in the near future. Plus, there are a number of articles in the "Spiritual Matters" topic that can help you grow in this area of your life.

PILLAR 2: BEING A TRUSTWORTHY PARTNER IS ESSENTIAL

"Many marriages lie in ruins because husbands and wives have lost sight of what is important: their spouse's trust."

- Paraphrase of E'yen A. Gardner
"Husband Rules: A Guy's Playbook on How to Win in Marriage"

Next to the Prayer Pillar, building trust is the second most important foundational piece in any marriage. For without it, as Gardner says, your marriage could lie in ruins. Over the years, Cindy and I have observed how trust is such a fragile matter. The more insecure a spouse is, the harder it is to establish a solid trust foundation in the marriage. We know this from personal experience.

When Cindy and I first started dating, I was extremely insecure and jealous. I was always suspicious that she would break up with me to be with another guy. Anytime I would see another guy even look at Cindy I instantly would get upset. My unfounded jealousy caused a lot of fights. Now, Cindy would also admit that she was a flirt during that time, but she had no ulterior motives of trying to hook up with someone else. Yet her occasional flirtations only added to my insecurities.

The longer we dated, her flirtations stopped (except with me), and I felt I could trust her more. So eventually my insecurities dissipated, but they didn't go away entirely. I would say they lay dormant. From time to time my jealousy would rear its ugly head, and I would say something to Cindy that was completely out of line. My outbursts and unkind comments caused a lot of problems.

Even after we became Christians there were times when a man would walk up to Cindy at church and start talking with her. When I spotted this, I would almost trip over myself to rush to Cindy's side. It was as though I was "marking my territory" subliminally and letting this "intruder" know that "she was mine" and to back off!

Of course, my display of immaturity always embarrassed Cindy and created tension between us. These displays were definitely not my finest moments as her husband. I also want to be clear that at this point in our marriage Cindy would never give off any signals (flirt) with another man. She saw our marriage vows as sacred. This was my issue.

Fortunately, I had some wise Christian men around me who helped me recognize that the enemy of our faith was trying to use my insecurity as a way to destroy trust in our marriage. Once that realization set in, I no longer felt threatened and I had unwavering trust in Cindy. She has done everything she can to show me that she is worthy of my trust. And for that, I am most grateful.

On the other side of the "trust coin," however, I was giving Cindy plenty of reasons not to trust me. This was due to my severe porn addiction. I would seesaw between complete abstinence and then "occasional" relapses. She knew my head was filled with countless images of airbrushed women from the time I was twelve years old. She felt there was no way she could ever measure up to what my imagination could conjure up about sex, and this created a deep insecurity within her.

There was absolutely no way I could ever convince her that I would never have a physical affair with another woman because I had already committed adultery in my head with these other women in the pictures. It's true what Jesus said in Matthew 5:28, NIV, "But I tell you that anyone who looks at a woman lustfully has already committed adultery with her in his heart."

This was an ongoing battle for me for years. What still amazes me to this day is the fact that Cindy not only stayed with me, she also helped me and supported my efforts to win the victory. I'll share more about how this happened and also what you can do if you're waging the battle for sexual purity in Marriage Essential #5.

But suffice it to say, God gave me the victory over that addiction, which strengthened the foundation for mutual trust that Cindy and I now enjoy with each other. We believe that as long as we continue to put Christ first in our lives, we will both remain worthy of trust. But we're not naïve; we both know we can still fall into temptation if we don't guard our hearts. (More on that in Essential #5.)

PILLAR 3: BE A PERSON OF INTEGRITY

> "The measure of a man's real character is what he would do if he would never be found out."
>
> - Thomas Macauley

The same can be said of a woman's real character. We believe that integrity and trust are inseparable in a successful marriage. "Integrity—The Key to Character and the Cure for Inconsistency" is an online article I found by Dr. Steven Riser that captures the key components of integrity that Cindy and I believe are crucial for us as believers to embrace if we're going to have a firm foundation in our marriages. Riser says:

> "Many people today view integrity as an outdated idea that is either expendable or no longer applicable in an age of moral relativism. Just as honesty is essential for trust and trust is essential for any healthy relationship and for the ability to lead, so integrity is essential to becoming trustworthy. It has been said that if you can't trust someone in all areas, you can't trust them in any. We compromise our integrity whenever we betray a trust. Integrity is a prerequisite to credibility. It involves an inner sense of wholeness, which results from being consistently honest and morally upright. Integrity is crucial in all aspects of life: professional, personal, social and spiritual."

He then goes on to give us a great definition, just so we're clear on this principle:

> "Among other definitions, Webster describes integrity as 'soundness of moral character.' Integrity from a biblical viewpoint has to do with being morally sound. What does it mean to be morally sound? A person with integrity knows what is important to God and consistently lives in light of what is important to Him. It involves more than living our values; it involves subscribing to God's values and with His help learning to conform our conduct to those values. Integrity is like the foundation of a house, if it is unstable, the entire house may come apart when it comes under pressure."

If you'd like to read the article in its entirety simply do an Internet search with "Dr. Steven Riser article on Integrity."

Integrity is modeled for us throughout the Bible, but two key illustrations for me have been Daniel, who could not be bought or forced to compromise in his beliefs and, of course, Jesus. One scripture verse sums it up for me after Jesus spent forty days in the desert face-to-face with the Devil: "For we do not have a high priest who is unable to sympathize with our weaknesses, but one who in every respect has been tempted as we are, yet without sin" (Hebrews 4:15, ESV).

If you are lacking the integrity your wife needs to feel secure in her trust for you, then please go to God in prayer. Believe me, He has a vested interest in your integrity and character, and He will help you—if you only ask.

Pillar 4: Make Sure You Are a Covenant-Keeper in Word and Deed

> "A covenant marriage is intended by God to be a lifelong relationship exemplifying unconditional love, reconciliation, sexual purity, and growth. A covenant is an eternal commitment with God. People can negotiate out of contracts, but not out of a covenant."
>
> - From www.CovenantMarriage.com

Most, if not all of us, repeated some vows at our wedding. If you were creative you wrote your own, while many of us recited the usual vows that have been given for hundreds of years. Here's what I said to Cindy on March 18, 1972:

> *I, Steven Keith Wright, do take you, Cynthia Denise Rowland, to be my lawfully wedded wife, to have and to hold from this day forward; for better for worse, for richer for poorer, in sickness and in health, to love and to cherish, till death us do part, according to God's holy ordinance; and thereto I pledge thee my troth. With this ring I thee wed: In the name of the Father, and of the Son, and of the Holy Ghost. Amen.*

It took less than five minutes for both Cindy and me to repeat our marriage vows. And honestly at that time... to me... it was just a legal ritual we had to go through so I could have sex, and live with Cindy. I didn't really stop to think about what each of those words really meant. But it didn't take long in our marriage before we both began to find out their real significance.

From the very beginning, we knew "poorer." I was a disc jockey at a small radio station, and Cindy worked part-time at my parents' art store. We barely made above minimum wage and we got paid every two weeks. By the end of the second week, we often had to dig through sofa and car seat cushions to try to scrape up enough change to buy a loaf of bread or quart of milk.

Then the "sickness" hit us between the eyes the second year into our marriage when I was diagnosed as a Type-1 diabetic. That also kicked in the "worse" part of marriage because of the personality changes I went through, plus our constant arguing over my health, and just about anything else that raised its ugly head in our circumstances.

Remember, at the time these difficult times hit us we weren't Christians; our foundation was very shaky to begin with. Looking back now we can see it was only because God somehow kept us together until we surrendered our lives to Him. But in the forty-three years since we became Christ-followers, we have still had the poorer, sickness, and worse times hit us hard at times. The difference is that we have not only survived—we have thrived because we are determined to be Covenant Keepers in our marriage.

In our marriage ministry today, we hear from hundreds of people every week. One of the things that disturb us greatly is when someone writes (usually a woman) and says her marriage is ending after being wed for only a few weeks. Sometimes it's only a matter of days after the wedding when one spouse will hear, "I made a mistake." The reasons are ridiculous. We know if it grieves our hearts, but it has to break God's heart even more.

Rarely today do you hear of a couple that make strong covenant vows. I read recently that of all marriages performed in the United States, only between 0.025–1 percent choose to have a Covenant Wedding. To find out more about this kind of wedding search for the term "covenant weddings" on the Internet.

If you didn't start your marriage as a Covenant Keeper, it's never too late to become a Covenant marriage. Maybe you have a 5th, 10th, 20th, etc., wedding anniversary coming up, and you want to renew your vows. This would be a great time to make it a Covenant wedding ceremony.

To help with clarity on the difference between promises and vows, here's what the Covenant Weddings website offers as a definition:

"Vows involve greater accountability and solemnity than do promises. I may promise to cook you dinner every night but because of certain circumstances that arise I may have to break that promise. On the other hand, if I vow before others that I will love and honor you all the days of my life, circumstances should not cause me to break this vow. I am also held to greater accountability by God and the community. Semantics? Possibly, but various cultures and traditions hold vows as sacred as compared to every day promises."

Here's a question I have for you: Do you hold the vows you made to each other as sacred? If you can't say "yes" to that, then we implore you to make it a matter of study and prayer to see how God reveals what He wants for your marriage.

One of the words in our vows that often are overlooked is the word "cherish." I know I didn't pay any attention to it until well into our marriage. The light finally came on for me as we were approaching our twentieth wedding anniversary. I wanted to show Cindy how much I loved and cherished her.

Four years earlier we had moved into a new house because of a ministry transfer to a new city. As Cindy was doing deep cleaning, she took off her wedding ring (we had matching gold bands, which were very unique). When she went back to where she was "sure" she placed it, it was gone.

From that moment on we searched, tore things apart, looking anywhere and everywhere we could think of—sink drains, heating vents, even emptying large garbage containers on the floor of the garage and going through each piece of trash (several times) in hot, humid weather. But all of our efforts were futile—the ring was gone. To say Cindy was crushed is an understatement. She mourned the loss of the ring every day... for years.

I offered to buy her a new ring to replace it—any ring she wanted—but she always declined, saying she only wanted her ring. One day I had a "light bulb" moment, where everything became clear as to how to solve that problem. You've heard of a "good idea..." I had a "God idea."

I wanted to find out if a duplicate of my wedding band could be made for Cindy that I could give to her on our twentieth wedding anniversary. So, I went to a jeweler, showed him my ring, and he said he could do it, but he would need my wedding band for two weeks in order to cast a mold to make an exact replica of the ring.

God Did the Impossible

How was I going to keep Cindy from noticing I didn't have my wedding ring on—for two weeks? I thought I might get away with it for a few days, but soon she was bound to notice. Cindy is one of the most observant people on the planet. She will notice a piece of lint on the floor at fifty paces and pick it up. I had to come up with a plausible story to tell her when — notice I didn't say "if" — she asked. What complicated coming up with a story even more is the fact she knows that in all the years we were married I never took off my ring.

There was only one way this could work. God would have to blind her to the fact I didn't have my wedding ring on. I knew God parted the Red Sea for Moses and the Israelites, but I wasn't convinced He could outwit my wife.

So whenever we were together for the next two weeks, I would have my left hand in my pants pocket as much as possible. When we were sitting on the sofa watching TV, I would make sure she only had access to my right hand to hold. When we were eating at a table, I would keep my left hand on my lap as much as possible.

Finally, the jeweler called and I picked up the new ring, which was a perfect match, and I was able to put my wedding band back on. My heart rate returned to normal. Thank You, Jesus!

Part Two of the Plan

But that was only half of the equation. How was I going to present the ring to her? I got another "God idea." I was going to surprise Cindy with a vow ceremony in front of family and friends on our anniversary. I enlisted the help of our pastor and a very close family friend. Because our anniversary fell on a Wednesday, and our church had a regular midweek service on Wednesdays, our pastor suggested that we do it that evening. He said when we walked into the sanctuary he would have the wedding march played, and as we walked down the aisle he would have us repeat our vows. Then, when he came to the part of the ring exchange, he would ask, "What symbol of your vows do you have?" At that moment I would present the ring to Cindy—and then repeat, "With this ring, I thee wed."

Our friend, Mary, said she would take care of putting together a reception after the ceremony. She also arranged to have a veil to put on Cindy when we walked into the church. So, now all I had to do was figure out a way to sneak Cindy to church when we agreed that we wouldn't go that evening. As far as she knew, we were just going to go out to a romantic dinner and then spend the night at a motel.

That night after dinner I told Cindy I had a surprise that I needed to drive to. I asked her to close her eyes and not look. 95% of people would most assuredly peek, but not Cindy. I knew I could trust her implicitly.

When I pulled into the church, I told her she could open her eyes. Then I told her we needed to go inside for just a minute because I had to get something from our friend.

She waited in the foyer as I went in to verify everything was set for the surprise ceremony. At the same time our friend, Mary, came up to Cindy with a beautiful veil in her hands and told Cindy there was a surprise waiting for her. To say Cindy was confused is an understatement. The next thing she knew we were standing in the back of the church. The wedding march began and I walked my bride down the aisle. As the ceremony began, Cindy looked out and saw many of our original wedding party as well as our oldest son, David, who came home from college for this special occasion. Half of our church family was there that evening, too, after the pastor told them what was going to happen.

It became very emotional at the part of the renewal vows when the pastor asked for the ring, and I presented Cindy with a new, exact replica of her original wedding band. And unlike our original vows, this is where I really began to understand what it meant to "cherish" my wife, and this is where Cindy began to feel cherished by me.

Now, you don't have to do something that elaborate to demonstrate how much you cherish your wife. Take my wife's brother, Rick, for example. As he and his wife were approaching their twentieth anniversary, they were planning on being with us in Arizona. So, his idea was we would all spend a couple of days at the Grand Canyon and then at sunrise on Sunday morning they would repeat their vows (with me officiating) on a rock overlooking the canyon. It was just the four of us, but that, too, was very romantic and demonstrated to his wife, Linda, how much he cherished her.

If we think of these four pillars as the supporting posts of a building, even the removal of only one of them would cause the building to collapse. They are all equally important to the foundation of any marriage. Most everything we put into our marriage will either strengthen or weaken the foundation. There's very little middle ground that can be termed as "neutral."

How important is it to have this kind of foundation? As I was writing this we received the following on our website from a woman who posted this prayer request:

> "Pray for the healing of our marriage during our separation right now. Pray that the Lord moves in both of us and restores our marriage. **Also, that we don't lose Christ as our foundation again** (emphasis added)."

In the remaining six marriage essentials of this resource, we will help you to strengthen your foundation so that it becomes virtually indestructible. We will be sharing from our experiences and the things God has taught both of us, as well as what we've seen work in others' marriages.

Our promise to you is that we will be transparent. We aren't going to try to sell you anything; though we will refer you to resources that we believe can help you, as they've helped us. Cindy and I thank you for giving us the honor and privilege of being a part of your marriage. We don't take this invitation into your life together lightly.

Here's our prayer for you:

Father God, as we move forward through the rest of this material, we pray that you will keep our hearts and minds open to what it is You want us to learn and take away from this. Jesus, we know the enemy of our faith will try to minimize the content and keep us from seeing Your truth. Cindy and I pray against this evil, in Jesus' name and through His blood. Our hope is that all our marriages will bring honor and glory to you. Amen.

Marriage Essential #2
BE INTENTIONAL
In Growing Your Love Relationship

Cindy wrote in a blog some time ago, "To fall in love is no big feat. But to continue in love—that's the challenge. However, without intentionality involved in growing your relationship, I'm afraid it's not likely your love will grow in a positive direction." So, in this chapter, we're going to share what we have learned about growing our own love relationship, and the intentionality it took. And then we'll help you transfer these principles into your marriage.

STEVE

I want to begin by telling you a true story that recently happened that will serve as the perfect illustration for explaining why this marriage essential is so vital.

Garden in the Desert

Cindy and I live in the desert southwest portion of the United States. Our soil (because we live near the mountains) is primarily caliche. A while back, I literally had to use a jackhammer to get through it to put in some patio stones. The only thing that grows in it naturally is weeds. For some strange reason, Cindy and I have had this desire for several years to put in a small garden and grow vegetables, primarily tomatoes.

We started exploring if this was possible, and if so, what would we have to do to have a garden? Our research showed that we could do it. I spent a week going back and forth to our home supply store and built two raised garden boxes. Next, I bought, hauled, and put in topsoil and organic manure in each box and mixed it all thoroughly. I felt I had achieved the proper soil-to-fertilizer ratio that would actually grow a tomato plant.

That was just the beginning. I now had to buy 100 feet of various sized tubes and emitters to install an irrigation system to keep the tomatoes alive through our blistering heat. That took another week because you can't just leave the tubes on top of the ground; they need to be buried. At least that's what I've been told (by Cindy).

Now we had to buy the tomato plants and put them in the ground. But how many? I thought six would be enough but Cindy wanted eleven. I know what you're thinking, "Gee, that seems like an awful lot of tomatoes for just two people." It would be if we didn't have a plan for them. Being married to Cindy for more than forty-six years, I've learned that she does nothing "randomly." She always has a plan.

Her/our plan, at least that's what I've been told (by Cindy) is that we will have a big crop of tomatoes. What we don't eat immediately, we'll dehydrate, and then can the rest for our future use. Our homegrown tomatoes are destined to become sauces, used in soups, and more, that they can be stored for a number of years. And what we can't use we will give away to bless our neighbors.

Right now our eleven tomato plants have been in the ground for forty-one days, and all of them have a LOT of green tomatoes on them. It looks like we'll have a bumper crop. It's funny how we go out every morning and look at them to see how they are doing. We're so proud of our "little ones" for doing so well. We've even eaten a few of the smaller cherry tomatoes that have ripened fast. And for you skeptics—yes, they do taste better than store-bought tomatoes.

The Marriage Garden

It's true what horticulturist Liberty Hyde Bailey wrote:

> "A garden requires patient labor and attention. Plants do not grow merely to satisfy ambitions or to fulfill good intentions. They thrive because someone expended effort on them."

Using my analogy above, I'd like for us to think for a few minutes of our marriage like a garden. I mean, think about it, didn't the original marriage begin in a garden?

For some strange reason, most of us seem to assume that after the wedding our love will just somehow magically grow stronger without any real effort being expended on our part. As husbands, we think if we remember to buy our wife a valentine's card/gift, birthday card/ gift and NEVER forget our anniversary, then we've fulfilled our "obligation" to demonstrate that we love our wives. It's like the old joke of when the wife asks her husband why he doesn't tell her that he loves her. His response, "I told you that I loved you on our wedding day; if anything changes, I'll tell you." But, if we're smart we should take Bailey's "Horticultural wisdom" and apply it to growing our love. These same principles apply to wives, as it does to husbands.

Let me suggest that if you want to grow a healthy and productive marriage, it's going to take a lot of the following: planning, work, time, money, unity, and self-sacrifice. And this will not happen through "good luck" or happenstance. There's only one way it can happen- through intentionality.

So, I'm going to address the husbands in this portion of the explanation to the marriage essential. But please take note, wives... a lot of this can be applied to your approach to marriage. Just glean through it, change pronouns when applicable, and apply what you can use.

Men, if you're not willing to do this, then stop reading here because the rest of this essential is for the guys who want to grow their love relationship into the best marriage possible.

Planning

For most of my earlier life, my modus operandi was a "fly-by-the-seat-of-my-pants" approach. I would take things as they came, because I am an "everything will just work out okay" kind of person. And as I said above, Cindy is a thorough planner. It's in her DNA. This introduced its share of confrontations and battles earlier into our marriage.

Now, I knew that it was a far better practice to plan things in our marriage than my method, but I was just stubborn (and immature) enough to fight her on it. What I'm talking about here ranged from planning something simple like helping to plan meals, to vacations, major renovations to the house, disciplining, and caring for our sons, to ministry opportunities. My immaturity meant Cindy had to shoulder far more responsibility than she ever should have. It was grossly unfair to her.

I have confessed this sin to Cindy and asked her forgiveness, which she has given me. Today, I'm much better at this (though, not perfect) because God woke me up to my irresponsibility. This led me to be intentional to changing my behavior, to grow our marriage so it is healthy, loving, and strong.

When it comes to planning, there are all kinds of tools available to help you do this in a way that works for you on the Marriage Missions website. Please use what you believe will work for you, but first "ask" God for His wisdom for your marriage. And then "seek" for what you can use (that takes being proactive and actually doing it). "Knock" at the doors available, and helpful doors will be "opened" to you. (See: Matthew 7:7-8.)

Work

If our goal is to be more like Christ in our marriages ("Husbands, love your wives as Christ loved the church and gave Himself up for her" Eph. 5:25-26, ESV)... that's something we have to plan to do and then work at. It's not going to happen by wishing or hoping for it. We have to work to become what she needs. And just so you know, I wouldn't try to sell you on this if it hadn't helped to grow our love. It involves a commitment on our part to that intentionality that we spoke about earlier.

If you are like me, you agree with this scripture in "principle," but it's entirely different to put it into our daily beliefs and behaviors towards our wives. Why? Well, for me I found the answer to that question when I read the book, "Discovering the Mind of a Woman" by Ken Nair. The heading on the book, "The Key to Becoming a Strong and Irresistible Husband" intrigued me. So I dug in, and the following is what I found.

Early in his book, Ken cleared up for me just "why" God created woman. It goes beyond producing children. For millennia, we have misinterpreted Genesis 2:18, where God says, "I will make him a help meet." I know I did. Here's what Ken says:

> "Basically, God is saying, 'After the Fall, I know you won't have a clue about what godliness is, so I'm providing you with a helper. This helper will provide you with a means of measuring whether or not you are becoming more like what I want you to be, spiritually alive and functional. Christ is your example and the way. Then as you become more Christlike, you will also be furnishing your wife with the leadership that provides an example worth following. Together you can reestablish the spirit-to-spirit relationship with God that was lost.'"

- p. 39

Ken also shared something he said to a woman in a counseling session that really grabbed me:

> "Is it such a terrible thing for a wife to be unwilling that her husband settle for anything less than what God desires for him? Christlikeness! If God designed a wife to help her husband be successful, would He design her to be satisfied with anything less than helping him become successfully Christlike?"

- pp. 136 137

After I read that, I circled it and wrote in caps above it, CINDY, which meant I finally realized that was one of the primary ways God uses her in our marriage. She is to not only be a marriage partner (just as I am hers), she is *my* marriage partner. She is my wife, but she also helps me be more like Christ. This empowers me to be a better husband, father, and man of God.

As I read that book, God revealed to me how Cindy thinks and what she feels, and I began to love her more and more. I saw her as God's daughter and I thought to myself, How does God want me to treat His daughter? I challenge you men to ask yourselves the same question.

If you want to gain much-needed insight into your wife so that you can become more Christlike in your marriage, then I strongly recommend purchasing Ken's book. I can't recommend it highly enough, simply based on how it changed our marriage. You can get it by going to our website, at www.Marriagemissions.com, and clicking the Amazon Window on the Home Page.

Time

There are no shortcuts! If you want to grow your love as a couple it will take time. Just like my tomatoes that need adequate amounts of water, sunshine, and fertilizer, they also just take time for them to grow to be healthy.

When I was younger I was extremely impatient. I was the King of Shortcuts to accomplish my goals. I'm sure a lot of this was caused by my ADHD that I have had since I was a kid… and haven't outgrown. I remember one of the very first marriage retreats Cindy and I went to; it was a Marriage Encounter Weekend.

I never said it out loud, but I remember thinking in the back of my mind, Okay, I can put a weekend into my marriage as long as it makes me the way Cindy *wants* me to be—a better husband—by the end of the weekend.

Did you catch any flaws in my thinking? Does this hit close to home for you? Also, this was long before I read Ken Nair's book.

When I found out we had to do a lot of letter-writing about our feelings, I started to sweat big time. The first writing assignment they gave to us was to go back to our room to write a love letter to our spouse. I don't remember exactly what I said (I'm pretty sure I said "I Love You") in my letter, but I do remember it was about three pages shorter than Cindy's letter to me.

Back then I had real self-confidence issues, which mistakenly led me to believe that I could never measure up to Cindy's writing abilities. However, what we've come to learn is that we just have different styles. Hers isn't "right" and mine is "wrong;" it's just different. This is something that can only be learned with time... working together to grow your love.

Over the years we have invested time into just about every marriage conference known to mankind: *Love & Respect* (twice); *A Weekend to Remember* (twice); *Laugh Your Way to a Better Marriage* (twice to the "live" conference and multiple times for the DVD conference). The list goes on. Why? It's because we both want to learn something new that can help us improve the great marriage we already have.

Some may think that's overkill, but we think it has been the best investment of time we could spend our lives doing. Sure, we could have done any number of other things (and we have over our forty-six plus years together), but those things come in at a distant second place compared to the spiritual health of our marriage. I also want to say that there was one BIG difference between the *Marriage Encounter Weekend* and the rest of the ones we've attended. I went with the attitude that I wanted to learn something new that would help me be more like Christ in my marriage.

Time Does Equal Love

See if you can relate to the following story: Cindy and I met and fell in love in college. In between classes and many other activities we were involved in, we spent every waking hour we could with each other. After going out on a three-to-four-hour date, we would go back to our dormitories and one of us would call the other. We would then spend multiple hours "just talking." Neither one of us wanted to hang up; we just wanted to hear the other's voice for as long as possible.

This was true all through our dating and engagement years. Not long after the wedding, other "things" started to crowd out our "alone time." Then after our sons arrived it was fortunate if we could squeeze in an hour or two a week. Life just happened and our special times together slowly disappeared.

Sound familiar? Why did I think that just because we were now married our love would continue to grow by "osmosis"? It's kind of like, "Well, I planted my tomato plants, and now they'll just grow on their own." That, of course, is not true. I need to water them several times a day, fertilize them, and make sure there are no weeds trying to choke them out (which all take time).

Well, the same is true in our marriages. I know time is a precious commodity. Each of us is given the exact number of hours and minutes every day. God in His wisdom designed it that way. He knew way before the beginning of time, as we know it, that humans, at this date in time, would be pressed in on every side to get things accomplished every day. So, why didn't He, say back in 2000, think "Hmmmmm, maybe I should increase the number of hours in the day so my creation will be able to get their stuff done? Should I give them twenty-six hours? Maybe thirty hours a day? That should help them out. Even so, I'm pretty sure they wouldn't squander their time if I did that."

Okay, I know I'm stretching it here, but I think we both know that even if God did give us thirty hours a day, we would still complain, "It isn't enough time to get everything done, let alone invest time in my marriage."

What it all boils down to are our priorities. What's most important? This goes back to my first point (planning), because I can tell you from personal experience, if you don't plan it (time together on a regular basis), then it ain't gonna happen; it's as simple as that.

I'm going to be so bold as to say that when you are in the busiest seasons of life, you also need to plan time to have sex. You say, "That doesn't sound very spontaneous or romantic." Okay, I'll give you that, but even planned time together can be just as fun and fulfilling.

When our sons were younger (before the age of ten), we would all have "Quiet Time" for about two hours on Sunday afternoons. They would each be in their rooms reading, playing with LEGO bricks, or something else. They needed to spend some time alone, being quiet. It helped all of us be gentler and kinder to one another. Cindy and I would also have our "Quiet Time" in our room. No LEGO bricks were involved.

Sometimes we would cuddle; sometimes we would nap; sometimes we would make love, and sometimes we'd do all three (I call that the perfect trifecta). By the time we got up, we felt our emotional and physical batteries had been recharged. And as a man, I felt that I could take on the world and whatever it could throw at me in the coming week. I used to say I felt that

I could charge hell with a squirt gun and defeat the Devil. A little bit too much testosterone, huh?

At the height of our busy lives back in the '90s I was working 50+ hours a week, Cindy had a part-time job, and both of our sons were in high school. We were busy, and we were struggling to connect when Cindy found an article in McCall's magazine called "The 22 Minute Date." (We have this posted on our website in the Communication Tools topic, for more details.)

Here it is in a nutshell: pick an evening where you can isolate yourselves from all distractions. Turn off the TV (and all other electronic media), shut off or don't answer any phones for twenty-two minutes. (This is the average length of a TV sitcom without commercials.)

Then sit across from each other in a location where other family members can't interrupt you. Set a timer for twenty-two minutes and then talk... talk about positive things in your life. This isn't the time to bring up problems or past hurts in your marriage. We have lots of free conversation starters on our website to help you get started.

What Cindy and I discovered was that once we got rolling, we didn't want to stop after the timer went off at twenty-two minutes. So, yes, even twenty (or twenty-two) minutes once or twice a week is a BIG step in the right direction of using your marital time wisely. Here's one last thought for you on this topic:

> "Sometimes couples complain that their time is limited because they're so busy. The good news is that you don't need to spend enormous amounts of time together to breed closeness and connection. Regular, brief get-togethers work too. Small changes in your schedule can make a huge difference. But don't leave 'rendezvousing' up to chance. Plan and schedule dates together. Marriage is serious business."
>
> - Michele Weiner-Davis

Money

You were probably thinking I was going to talk about how important it is to spend money on your spouse to show them you "truly" love them. So, for those of you who thought this... yes, you need to spend money on your spouse from time to time to demonstrate that you love them. But that's not really what I want to focus on here. I want to focus on how you both view the use of money in your marriage. Because, believe it or not, when you learn to come together on how you use and view money, it will help to grow your love relationship immensely.

Most experts agree that the number one cause for strife in marriage is over money; plus, it is a leading cause of divorce. Cindy and I have come to understand that the primary reason for that is because we all come into the marriage with different backgrounds in what we learned about money in our homes of origin (how we grew up). Almost always one spouse could be called the spender (that was me) and the other the saver (that is Cindy). One isn't better than the other. In fact, they bring balance into the marriage relationship if they work together. Here's what Dr. Gary Chapman says on this issue:

> "Money was designed to be our servant, never our master. It's to be used to build our marriage and family and to honor God. Getting a proper perspective on money is the first step to solving financial conflicts. [To the best of your ability] become equal partners. The second step relates to whether you handle money as partners or competitors. There's no room for competition in marriage; you and your mate are equal partners on the same team. Certainly, one partner will need to pay the monthly bills and balance the bank statement. But this doesn't mean the bookkeeper controls the money. Together you must develop a plan for processing your finances. The bookkeeper simply follows the plan to which you've both agreed."
>
> - www.todayschristianwoman.com
> Article, "Balancing Your Money Mindset"

Below are nineteen questions every couple needs to ask each other. It's always better to do this before you marry, but it's also never too late to start. Begin working together on managing your money wisely.

Before you ever do this, make sure you pray first. Pray that God would give you a unified heart. I can promise you this won't necessarily be easy to do in the beginning; it wasn't for us.

You need to remember that as Dr. Chapman said, money "...is to be used to build our marriage and family to honor God." If you find yourselves starting to get heated or in complete disagreement, take a break and come back later when things have cooled down.

And then, here are a few questions to discuss together:

1. Who's going to pay our monthly bills in our household?
2. Who's going to balance the bank statement each month?
3. What are your feelings about joint versus separate checking accounts?
4. What do you think about credit cards? Which cards should we keep (if any)?
5. Do you see yourself as "good with keeping books" or "bad with keeping books?"
6. Will our income support the standard of living we want to have? If not, what adjustments do we need to make?
7. What are your feelings about a monthly budget?
8. What are your feelings about a will? When do you think we should have one made? Why?
9. How much money should we spend a year on luxury items, such as jewelry, athletic, or electronic equipment, trips, etc.?
10. How do you feel about borrowing money from our parents or relatives?
11. How do you feel about loaning money to our parents or relatives?
12. What percent of our income should we give to the place of worship we attend? Why?
13. What percent of our income should we give to charitable organizations? Which ones?
14. How much life insurance should we have? Health insurance? What company? Why?
15. Do you want to invest some of our money? How? When?
16. How much should we spend on a getaway weekend?
17. How would you have the most amount of fun if we only have five dollars to spend some evening?

18. How much should we spend on special occasions such as:

    - Birthdays: each other's, parents, children, friends, others
    - Anniversaries: our own; parents, friends, relatives, others
    - Other special days: Mother's Day, Father's Day, Valentine's Day
    - Christmas: each other's gift, parents, children, other relatives, co-workers, friends, and decorations?

19. What should be the dollar limit on purchases made without the other's knowledge? Why?

> \- Bobb and Cheryl Bieh
> "Making the Most of Your Honeymoon Year"
> no longer in print
> For more information go to www.Bobbbiehl.com
> Used by permission

These nineteen questions are by no means exhaustive when it comes to what we need to talk about, and come to agreement on, our finances. But they are a good start. Remember, there are so many tools available on the web to help you put budgets together and manage your money and reduce tension in your marriage.

Unity

> "Haven't you read," [Jesus] replied, "that at the beginning the Creator 'made them male and female,' and said, 'For this reason a man will leave his father and mother and be united to his wife, and the two will become one flesh'? So they are no longer two, but one flesh. Therefore what God has joined together, let no one separate."
>
> \- Matthew 19:4-6
> NIV

These verses are read at nearly every Christian wedding ceremony. Most, if not all of us, entered into our marriage with the proclamation that the two of us would become "one flesh." If so, then why do so many of us end up divorcing? Cindy and I believe it boils down to just one thing: we have taken our eyes off of what is supposed to bring unity to our marriage.

"Unity in marriage is simple conceptually. Only one thing is necessary: a mutual commitment to the Lord and his glory."

- Tim Savage
"No Ordinary Marriage"

It took us a while in our relationship to come to the full understanding of how important this is. But we can honestly say if it wasn't for the fact that we both have been committed to the "Lord and His Glory," we could easily have thrown in the towel many times. We don't pretend this is easy to do and keep at the forefront of our thoughts, especially when we find ourselves arguing over something. But it's amazing how every time we've gotten into a heated argument, God always convicts both of us to the point where we see we have taken our eyes off of Him. Instead, we have been busy focusing on our wants—our needs. Once that happens, it brings us back together to seek reconciliation and understanding.

Why Unity Is So Important

I serve as the chaplain for the fire department in our community. Some of my duties include being called to the scene when someone has died and a surviving family member asks for a chaplain. I was on such a call recently. This particular couple had been married nearly fifty-six years. The husband, who was eight-seven, had been ill for several years and died in his sleep; so it didn't come as a shock to his widow. I sat with her for a while and mourned with her.

Then she got up and walked into the bedroom where his body lay (waiting for the coroner to arrive) and sat down next to him. For the longest time, she talked to him, stroked his forehead, held his hand and cried occasionally. She told him she loved him over and over.

I left her alone for about thirty minutes to mourn privately, and then I asked if I could join her. So, I sat with her and asked her to tell me how they met, fell in love, got married, and about their long life together as a married couple.

In spite of her grief, her eyes sparkled as she shared about these fond memories and treasured experiences. She then pointed to a picture on her nightstand and said it was her favorite. I walked over to look at it. It was a black-and-white picture taken of her and her husband through the back window of the car as they drove away on their honeymoon. Their faces were radiating love and hope.

What I came away from that time with was this couple had loved each other deeply and that they stuck it out through the good times as well as the bad. And today—when their earthly marriage ended—the legacy of that marriage to their kids and everyone who knew them was an example of what C. S. Lewis said:

> "Love as distinct from 'being in love' is not merely a feeling. It is a deep unity, maintained by the will and deliberately strengthened by habit; reinforced by the grace which both partners ask, and receive from God. They can have this love for each other even at those moments when they do not like each other; as you love yourself even when you do not like yourself."
>
> - C. S. Lewis
> "Mere Christianity"

Have you ever asked yourself, "What image do people see in us as a married couple? Do they see the image of God lived out in us; or do they see something entirely different that would repulse them from wanting to know our God?"

Well, Lewis gives us a great exhortation on how we can achieve the unity God desires for our marriages. In summary, marital unity starts with God; it is maintained through God (for as long as we both shall live), so when we come to the end of our lives God will get the glory for the way we lived out our marriage trusting in Him.

Self Sacrifice

If you have spent any amount of time studying the Bible, you know one of the major themes repeated throughout Scripture is the need for self-sacrifice. I did an Internet search on the "number of Bible verses on self-sacrifice" and came up with forty-nine references. The way I figure it, if God mentions something more than once in the Bible, I better pay attention to what He is saying.

I'm not saying if something is mentioned only "once" we don't need to pay attention to it. Of course you should!

Another way to grow by leaps and bounds in our love relationship within our marriages is to practice self-sacrifice every day. Author Al Jansen, in his book "The Marriage Masterpiece" says that the meaning of marriage is not found in "pursuing self-fulfillment;" rather, the meaning in marriage is obtained by "practicing self-sacrifice."

Al also says we husbands have many opportunities every single day to give up what we want to do and instead serve our wives. He gave a few examples of how we can put this into action:

- Biting my tongue when I want to defend myself from what she said.
- Getting up in the middle of the night when a child cries rather than pretending I don't hear anything.
- Putting down my reading material and really listening when she wants to talk.
- Taking over some chores when she's got a hectic day.
- Cleaning the kitchen Sunday evening rather than leaving the mess for her to face on Monday morning.
- When I'm accidentally exposed to porn while channel surfing in a hotel room far from home, I shut off the television because I won't allow any impure thoughts to invade my marriage.

Truly, the list could go on and on, but this gives us some practical ways to start implementing a lifestyle of self-sacrifice for our wives.

If this seems overwhelming, take just one point per day to meditate on, and ask God how He wants to use it in your life. I can almost guarantee your love relationship will grow.

In Marriage Essential #1, I wrote about building strong foundations for your marriage. I also wrote about tearing down shaky foundations that are faulty. I confessed that Steve and I had to do that. We had built the foundation of our marriage on unrealistic, idealistic love, or what we thought was love. But for our marriage to survive and then grow and mature, we had to tear down the shaky foundation we had built. And then we had to build a stronger one that honors God's approach to marriage.

From that stance of building upon a stronger foundation, God showed us that what we were experiencing earlier in our marriage really wasn't love lived out at all. It was our idea of love. It was actually love wrapped up in "selfism." We were more in love with our interpretation of love than with each other. This consisted of how the other made us feel about ourselves. And yes, that is important. But it isn't supposed to be the total basis for marital love.

The longevity of marriage demands more from us than that ego-centered image of love. It's God's agape (wanting the best for the other person) type of love that helps us stay together through good and the tough times. We are to lovingly persevere, not as the "world" loves, but as God loves. As we do that, we are able to grow our love relationship.

Something that John Thomas wrote on this issue is important to note:

> "Sadly, most Christian marriages represent nothing more than re-packaged psychology. It is Hollywood nonsense wrapped in a few Bible verses, with a vision so low it's no wonder half of them end in divorce."
>
> - Boundless.org
> Article, "The Sacrifices of Marriage"

That is a lot to take in when you think about it.

Lord, help us to love, within our marriages, as You would have us, rather than loving as the world does with "re-packaged psychology."

Getting Needs Met

John Thomas then says the following that I also agree with:

> "How I long for Christ-followers to experience the stunning views of God from the top of the peak of marriage! Unfortunately, most are stuck in the climb, whining and complaining about not getting his or her 'needs met,' which is for each of them the highest goal of marriage."
>
> - Boundless.org
> Article, "The Sacrifices of Marriage"

Yes, we do marry to get a lot of our needs met—especially the need for "loving togetherness." That makes sense, and it's important. But I believe whole-heartedly that God wants to grow us through this journey called marriage. It isn't all about us and having our needs met that is most important. There is a question that challenges this premise. It's one that author Gary Thomas poses: "What if God designed marriage to make us holy more than to make us happy?"

This challenging question is supported by what is written about love and marriage in the Bible. According to Scripture, we are to consider each other as more important than ourselves. And we are to participate with God in His Kingdom work, above our own work and comforts. All of this takes intentionality in lining up our attitudes and our actions with God's higher ways. It also requires the willingness to humble ourselves so that we can accept His grace and grow in our love for our spouse. And sometimes growth comes through painful times.

Let's face it... we don't grow as deeply spiritually and emotionally when everything is going along smoothly. In our humanness, we seem to need to be stretched beyond our comfort zones at times. And just as "iron sharpens iron" (Proverbs 27:17), so does our spouse sharpen us when he or she rubs us emotionally in ways that aren't comfortable. Sometimes it's downright painful. But it can also help us to grow in ways we may never have grown otherwise.

Steve and I have gone through some very painful times. But those have also been times when we have grown the most, as we come out on the other end.

Be Growth-Focused

God has been teaching Steve and me to be growth-focused in our approach to marriage more than "me" or "problem-focused." I like what Carrie Oliver pointed out about this concept. She wrote, in "a growth-focused marriage":

> "Couples identify problems but don't dwell on them. They look beyond the solutions to how God might use this process to teach them more about Him and/or themselves, their partners, and their marriages. They understand problems are inevitable. The real challenge is in dealing with them in such a way that honors God and each other while helping the couple grow through it."
>
> - www.crosswalk.com
> Article, "Ready, Set, Grow"

Growth doesn't happen without feeding that which we want to grow (and pulling out the weeds that could choke out the good). For that to happen we must be proactive. We must do something on purpose to achieve a wanted goal. In this case, it is growing love in our marriage relationship by showing love in little and big ways. This grows the warmth we feel towards each other.

True Love vs. Surface Love

But love, true love, demands more of a person than hopping from one little sunshine moment of pleasure to another and another. Sure, those warm moments are important to enjoy within marriage too. But they aren't sustainable for making it through the big issues that sometimes suddenly creep into our lives unexpected. Surface "love" never plumbs to the depths of what it is to show love to someone who isn't showing love in return. And it doesn't serve the other spouse with a gracious attitude when they are tired—when they don't want to do what they could or should do. Yet when the tables are turned, we sure want that gracious attitude extended to us when we're tired. So why should we give our spouse any less?

Several years ago, a Christian couple won the "Happy Marriage" contest. What they wrote was published in the June 1996 issue of Good Housekeeping Magazine. What was their secret?

> "We gave when we wanted to receive; we served when we wanted to feast. We shared when we wanted to keep. We listened when we wanted to talk, and we submitted when we wanted to reign. Each of us forgave when we wanted to remember, and we stayed when we wanted to leave."

Great advice, huh? Please know that "Romance starts in the heart—with a servant's heart" (Annie Chapman). "You... were called to be free. But do not use your freedom to indulge the sinful nature. Rather serve one another in love." (Galatians 5:13, ESV).

I wrote a bit about this in a blog a while ago. In it, I talked about "Love in Action," which can help to grow our love relationship with each other. In my own marriage, and maybe you can relate to this by thinking of incidences in your own marriage... I've come to realize that:

- When Steve is sick and I have to shoulder more of the load of things that need to get done, even though I'm exhausted, and yet I do it anyway... that is love in action.

- Love in action is exhibited when Steve is patient with me, despite my bad attitude. It's when he decides not to give in and argue with me. Yet instead, he gives me grace and space to work through whatever I'm dealing with. He sometimes even gives me a hug even though I'm not very huggable at that time.

- When Steve leaves his insulin or his cell phone at home and I drive it to where he is working that day—that is love in action. I do this even though it is totally inconvenient to my schedule. But showing love to our spouse isn't usually based on convenience. It's just what you do, despite what your emotions are saying.

- Love in action is when Steve rubs my feet when they are hurting after I've been on them too long. He does this even though that can't be the most pleasant thing to do. (Thank you, Steve.)

- Love in action is shown when Steve is talking to someone and I want so badly to say, "That's not the way it was… " but I don't. I decide to leave his dignity intact. If it's important, we talk about it later. But for now (or maybe forever), I leave it alone.
- When Steve wants to finish off a dessert all by himself but offers the rest to me instead… that is love in action.
- And when I say, "No, you have the rest of your dessert; I'm fine," even though I want it SO badly… that is love in action. (We usually split it at that point, but sometimes not.)
- When a scantily clothed gal comes on a television commercial and Steve turns away, and intentionally does not look… that is love in action. I know he is tempted. But he chooses to honor me and honor God by not going the way of temptation. Oh, how I love that. It makes me feel truly loved and cherished!
- Love in action is when I shorten a very long story I'm telling as I see my husband's eyes glazing over. I want to share more, but I perceive that his ears need a rest. So I honor that by being brief (and saving my longer story for a gal friend who would appreciate the details).
- Another point of love in action happens when Steve doesn't brag that he is able to write the additions to his 7 Essentials for this marriage guide faster than me.
- And when I catch up, and surpass him, love in action requires that I don't brag about it.
- When Steve doesn't bring up a past failure of mine, or I don't bring up one of his, we are giving grace and love.

I think you get the point of all of these actions… They are 1 Corinthians 13 lived out in real life. THAT is real love. It ditches the "selfie mindset" and lives out sacrificial love, as Christ did for us. He gave the ultimate love in action when He sacrificed Himself on the cross for us, even though we turn our back on Him in different ways. He is our greatest example.

> "When Jesus saw us hopelessly enslaved to sin, he didn't say, 'I don't feel like dying on a cross for them. I think I'll wait until the feeling comes.' He didn't say, 'I've tried and tried to love them but they always reject me. I give up!' Jesus acted lovingly toward us despite our rejecting Him. His love didn't

depend on what we did to deserve it, or even on whether we accepted it. Jesus freely gave us his love. This is how God wants us to love our spouses."

- Henry Blackaby
"The Experience: Day by Day with God: A Devotional and Journal"

All of what I describe is love in action. Sometimes words go with them... sometimes not. Expressing love verbally is an important piece of a healthy marriage built on God's foundational principles. But actions speak even louder than words in these incidences. Perhaps you can think of some of your own. Don't just think of what you do, but try to think of some of what your spouse does for you. It could make you appreciate him or her more.

Showing Appreciation

Some of these actions are ones that can easily go unrecognized. They are actions that the other spouse can often take for granted. I'm talking about the unappreciated spouse who faithfully goes to work to help support the family financially. I'm talking about a spouse who is faithful, even though they are faced with temptation at every turn. (This is not a very marriage-friendly world, even though it pretends to be.) Sometimes a spouse is taken for granted who regularly puts gas in the car, mows the lawn, does the dishes, vacuums, pays the bills, takes care of the kid's needs, and/or does the laundry... the list goes on. Sometimes it's the wife who does these things, and sometimes it's the husband who does them. But regardless of who does them, words of appreciation, given by the other spouse, will go a long way in growing a marital love relationship.

What is my point? Amplify your love and appreciation with your words.

Sure, you might expect these things from your spouse, and he or she can expect them from you. But giving a hug and saying thanks for everyday things that no one else may notice gives your spouse a type of paycheck of the heart that is priceless. It helps your spouse to not feel that he or she is taken for granted. Invest in your marriage relationship. Make sure your spouse knows that he or she is your top priority, after God.

> "Your spouse needs to come to the top of your priority list—just a bubble behind Jesus. You need to give your spouse priority access to your time—instead of just the leftovers."

- Drs. Gary and Barb Rosberg

Show love and appreciation by what you say, what you do, and how you make time to spend quality time together. The efforts you make to invest in your marriage can grow your love relationship in exponential ways. Saying your wedding vows to each other did not erase either of your needs to feel loved and appreciated. Please know that.

> "If you've been ignoring a taking-my-spouse-for-granted weed, pull it up now and fill the gaping hole with flowers of appreciation or thoughtful words of gratitude. If you're stuck for words, close your eyes and imagine what you would have said in your courting days. Digging deep into that well will bring up sweet water."
>
> - Alistair Begg
www.familylife.com
Article, "3 Weeds to Pull From Your Marriage Garden"

Also, saying nice things about our spouse to a family member, a friend, or even a stranger in front of your spouse can mean a lot to him or her. It's been said that, "Giving accolades in front of an audience is like giving care packages for the heart." This is a sure way to grow your love relationship with your spouse. I've seen this to be true in my own marriage and in hundreds of marriages that we've observed. Who doesn't like to be bragged on—especially by our spouse?

Another intentional essential to grow your love relationship is to:

Be Present With; Be Attuned to Your Spouse

A number of years ago Steve and I heard Pat Love, who is a relationship expert, speak on basic keys to loving. She gave two points (among several) that I'd like to pass on to you on this subject of being intentional in growing your love relationship. One of these points is:

> "You've got to show up. You've got to be present. You've got to log in some hours with each other."

You didn't marry each other for the main reason of building a home, a career, and/or have some kids. You married to be with each other. The other reasons are to come up behind that one—other than glorifying God together. You had a love relationship in the first place, which made you want to get married to this special person. But now you need to grow this love relationship so it doesn't die from lack of attention. Love doesn't do well growing on a starvation diet. It needs your attention pointed towards each other in positive ways.

It doesn't make sense to have our marriage partner dying of loneliness, living in the same house with us, while we spend time with everything and everyone else. And that's what is happening in a lot of marriages. Please don't allow your marriage to be one of them.

> "Love does not die easily. It is a living thing. It thrives in the face of most of life's hazards, save one—neglect."
>
> - James Bryden

We can say our spouse is a top priority, but do we show them that by scheduling time to spend with them?

Even giving them snippets of time here and there is better than spending little or no time together. Please know that we have a topic on the Marriage Missions website (that we regularly add to) devoted to "Romantic Ideas." These include "Cheap Dates for You and Your Mate" and all kinds of romantic things you can do together. So, show up; put intentionality into logging in some quality hours together to grow your love relationship with each other.

It's like what author Pat Williams testified of their marriage when it was in trouble. He wrote:

> "The trouble in our marriage wasn't infidelity, it was fidelity with fatigue, a marriage gone soft and sour due to lack of attention. It was the lack of communication that nearly killed us."

Don't let this happen to you. Be there for each other and grow your love.

A Second "Key to Loving"

Another point that Pat Love made as far as a basic key to a loving relationship is:

> "You've got to tune in."

Be present with each other, and tune in when you are. As Pat said,

> "Attunement means that when I'm present with you, I am not multitasking... You cannot be intimate when you're multitasking."

As we're told in the Bible, there is "a time for everything under Heaven." But when you are with your spouse, do your best to put your multitasking aside whenever you can.

This is a difficult one for me. I'm all about multitasking. It's what I do continually. The exceptions are when I'm spending one-on-one time with God and one-on-one time with Steve, or with family members or friends. I try to be aware of giving them my undivided attention whenever possible. I know that's important. Oh yeah, and then there's sleep time. But the rest of the time... I'm all over the place doing... and doing. Steve often jokes about that. But in all seriousness, he is secure in the concentrated time I spend with him.

Giving concentrated time to your spouse is absolutely crucial if you are going to grow your love relationship.

Regarding this issue, I want to tell you about a pet peeve of mine. It concerns the time we spend connecting on social media, at the expense of being with our spouse.

I have a love/hate relationship with computers, media devices, and cell phones. They are the greatest inventions, and yet they are the worst. I love the info and connection time you can gain through them with a whole world of people and data. BUT there can also be the illusion of connection going on, as well. You can text and text with everyone under the sun, but little bits of info typed out does not make the connection deep. And in the meantime, you can often neglect your spouse who is sitting right next to you or is in the next room and needs your attention.

Connect in Person

When I walk into a restaurant and I see couples and family members sitting together, and yet they are texting or talking on their phones, I go a bit crazy. There is a time and place for everything. But when we are with others, we need to be present with them! Yes, there are exceptions, but that's what they should be: Rare exceptions. Tune into your spouse when you are out with your spouse.

Steve and I were at a restaurant the other day where a family of four was sitting at the next table. The wife/mom was on her phone texting away. The husband/father was on his phone getting some kind of info from it. The older son was playing a video game on his phone. And there was a little girl, probably about six or so, who was bored to no end. She was bouncing around trying to get their attention, but to no avail. What a sad picture this was to watch! Here was a beautiful family all "connected" somewhere else, but not with one another. It made me want to cry.

Connecting in person—giving your marriage partner your focused attention whenever possible—is one of the greatest everyday gifts you can give to them. By focused attention I mean:

- Look into your spouse's eyes to connect when he or she talks to you.

- Make sure you actively listen to what your spouse says to you. Don't appear to listen when, in reality, you're actually occupied with your thoughts and actions with something else.

- Make sure your body language says "I care" when your spouse needs your attention. Don't be occupied with something else. Center your attention upon and interact with your spouse with your full attention.

- And here's a little bonus. It's something else that can cause your spouse to feel valued:

    Extend common courtesies to your spouse beyond what you do with other people. Remember your manners; be polite. Yes, you live together and you can't always be free of noises and smells, but try to do your best. Saying "Please" and "thank you" and "excuse me" goes a long way.

Show love, pursue love with your spouse, and then you will grow your love—a love that is lasting.

"Long-lasting love doesn't happen by accident. We don't find ourselves holding hands after twenty-five years with the one that we love by pure chance. Love is deliberate; it's intentional, it's purposeful, and in the end, it's worth every minute (and every effort) that we invest."

- Darlene Schacht

In growing your love relationship, become students of love.

"Watch what God does, and then you do it, like children who learn proper behavior from their parents. Mostly what God does is love you. Keep company with him and learn a life of love. Observe how Christ loved us. His love was not cautious but extravagant. He didn't love in order to get something from us but to give everything of himself to us. Love like that."

- Ephesians 5:1-2,
The Message

MARRIAGE ESSENTIAL #3
RENVIGORATING YOUR ROMANCE AND SEX LIFE

A lot of people think that the only way to invigorate or reinvigorate their marriage is to find ways to make their romantic feelings "sizzle" again. That can be true, but actually, it's more a matter of imparting strength and vitality back into the marriage. This may not sound exciting, but the results can be life-changing. Below are the ways we have found that work well in accomplishing this.

STEVE

When Cindy and I started the Marriage Missions International website seventeen years ago, we had no idea what would bring people to our site to look for help in their marriages. Our mission has been to "Reveal and reflect the heart of Christ within marriage" by providing Christ-centered marriage information on a variety of topics. We don't provide counseling or therapy. But we do provide info from a variety of "marriage experts" plus our own experience, and other people who post comments under each article. Some of their advice is actually better than that of the experts.

Well, we sure hit a nerve when we started writing and adding articles on topics relating to sex and romance. We discovered people from around the world were hungry for information on these subjects from a Biblical standpoint. Every week we get a detailed report on our website activity showing what the most viewed articles/topics have been. Invariably, the number one article with the most hits is: "Wife Does Not Want Sex," then in no particular order, the other top viewed topics every week are: "How Much Sex Is Normal" also, "Husband's Sexual Needs: Man or Monster," as well as, "When You Don't Want Sex With Your Husband," and "What Is Not Okay in Bed."

What we write about in this essential is not intended to be all-inclusive information to solve every issue you may be confronting in this sensitive and intimate area of your marriage. Rather, we hope to provide you with some ideas on how you can improve this area of your marriage. We are making an assumption that you both want to do better in this area, just as we did a number of years ago. That's why we call this section "Invigorate Your Romance and Sex Life With Each Other" and not, "Fixing Your Romance and Sex Life With Each Other."

I'm going to use an illustration to make my points. Hopefully, this will resonate with you. I want us to think of three links in a chain. The first link is Romance; the second link is Intimacy, and the third link is Sex.

Link 1: Romance

I hate to burst your bubble, men, but if you want to invigorate the "sex" part of your relationship, you must learn to romance your wife first. I didn't make up this rule; I learned it the hard way by not following it at first. And then through trial and error, and actually studying up on marital romance, I learned that God has wired our wives to need this. Also, as a Christian husband, I feel it is my responsibility to "Love my wife as Christ loved the church and gave Himself up for her." (Ephesians 5:25, ESV)

Here's how I interpret this relating to my sexual wants/needs in our relationship... I give up my instincts/wants/desires to first meet my wife's wants/desires; that is, she wants to be romanced to feel loved before she wants to make love. And from all the interactions Cindy and I have had with thousands of couples that have come to our website over the years, 99.5 percent of all women would agree.

See how I gave room for the few women on the planet who would disagree with this premise? Cindy and I know nothing is 100 percent.

And interestingly enough, there are those very rare times that the husband is the king of romance, when most likely he's married to a woman who doesn't really care for it.

Sadly, very few of us husbands today ever had a healthy romance modeled for us as we were growing up. My parents were married for forty-three years before my mom died, so I had the example of a marriage that stood the test of time. But I can't remember ever seeing my dad romance my mom. It was a foreign concept to me. However, after marrying Cindy I learned quickly what romance wasn't.

It wasn't coming home from work after she had spent the entire day with two toddlers changing diapers, wiping runny noses, cleaning the house, cooking meals, and looking at her saying, "Hubba, Hubba, Hubba, Baby. You sure look 'HOT' tonight!" That's NOT romance. That's the equivalent of dumping a bucket of ice water over her head, patting her on the backside, and saying, "So, when's dinner ready, darlin'? I'll be in the den watching TV."

WARNING TO MEN: If you ever do try this, I caution you to not turn your back on your wife—especially if there's something she can throw within her reach, and she has a good aim.

Honestly, romance perplexed me, and the first 10+ years we were married there were very few books that could help me get a handle on it. One of the first books that tackled this subject in the '90s was, *Sex Begins in the Kitchen*, written by Dr. Kevin Leman. This book has sold millions of copies and is in its fourth printing.

Leman explains how sexual intimacy is an expression of the care a couple shows each other in all areas of life—in communicating, sharing thoughts and feelings, and even in helping out around the house. Kevin is a master at giving insight with great humor that shows couples how to create new joy and excitement in their relationships. It's a good read.

Even though we may not have had good examples of this when we were growing up, there is so much available today that there is almost no excuse for you not to have a great "romantic" marriage, which leaves you both feeling satisfied. Cindy and I often say, "If you didn't have any good examples, then become a good example for others to follow."

We make an entire topic, "Romantic Ideas," available on our website with a number of different articles. There are also testimonies from other couples who have found the secret to what many of us thought was a perplexing subject. Let me give you few quick tips from just one article:

- **Be a man of God**. One of the best things that you can do to fire up romance is to become more like Jesus.
- **Be an awesome father**. Another way to really turn your wife's knees to Jell-O is to be an awesome father.
- **Get Dishpan Hands**. Some women think that the sexiest thing on a man is dishpan hands, so dive in and offer to do some extra household chores for your wife. This affirms Kevin Leman's Sex Begins in the Kitchen principle.
- **Watch a "Chick Flick."** (i.e., romantic movie). Ask her to choose. If you watch one of these movies and actually put effort into enjoying it, your wife will appreciate it.
- **Listen to Her**. Talk to your wife. Spend time together talking. Listening does not just mean listening to her words. It means valuing her opinions and letting her express herself.
- **Give Her a Massage**. Some women love to have a nice massage. I am not talking about the sexual kind of massage here. I am talking about a deep massage of the back, shoulders, neck, hands, and feet. Keep your hand off of anything that would be covered by a bikini. If she

wants to make love afterward, great! But let it be her idea.

- K. H., formerly featured on the website, www.CovenantSpice.com
Article, "How to Romantically Make Love to Your Wife"

Over the years I have put into practice every single one of these principles, and I can testify that they do work. The thing we have to remember, men, is that we have to be consistent and sincere. Our wives can tell if we're just "posers" trying to get them into bed.

What I discovered was the real power behind the first principle—be a man of God. Because the more I strive to be like Jesus, the rest of these principles become a delight for me to live out. And in turn, Cindy is delighted as well.

Link 2: Intimacy

"Intimacy should not be equated with sex. In fact, chances are, if you aren't intimate in the other areas of your life your sexual intimacy will be one of the first things to suffer."

- www.Marriageandfamilytoday.com
Article, "Marriage Life, Intimacy Is a Marathon Not a Sprint"

If given the choice between swimming across a pool filled with hungry crocodiles or talking about intimacy with is wife, most men would rather jump into the pool. But really, if we just look at what intimacy means, it shouldn't be that scary to us. The Oxford Dictionary defines intimacy as: "closeness, togetherness, affinity, rapport, attachment, familiarity, friendship, affection, warmth, confidence."

I can tell you that Cindy and I have every one of these active in our life today. But it didn't just happen. These attributes come from being intentional in cultivating them over time. If you've been married less than five years, you probably aren't experiencing these at any great depth. Be patient. Keep working on them, because they will develop.

Now, if you've been married for more than ten years and you still have major deficiencies in some or all of these areas, then you need to get off your backside and get to work. The rewards for doing so can be incalculable.

Understand that the more you work on romance, the more intimacy will grow; and the more you work on building intimacy, the more your romance quotient will go up. They are directly linked.

Think on These Things

Intimacy Killers (In no particular order):

> Dishonesty and Silence... Lack of Trust... Not Listening... Self-Centeredness... Lack of Respect... Past Sexual Abuse (unresolved)... Any Kind of Sexual Addiction (not being treated)... Unhealthy Arguments... Extreme Separateness... Putting Kids Ahead of Marriage. Also, one expert suggests, Smartphones, romance novels, and not wearing your wedding ring. This is by no means an exhaustive list, but it does give you a place to start checking what may be affecting intimacy in your marriage...

Intimacy Builders (In no particular order):

> Laughing Together... Encouraging Each Other... Touching Each Other (nonsexually)... Talking About Your Feelings... Forgiving and Being Forgiven... Protecting Your Image of Your Spouse."
>
> - Stephen Arterburn and Sam Gullucci
Excerpt from "Road Warrior"

If you would like to have a list of *100 Ways to Love Your Wife Her Way* (Intimacy builders), you can print off a list from our website. And to make things really easy for you, take the list to your wife and ask her to circle three things on the list that she would like to see you do in the next week. *Then do them!*

For wives we have *100 Ways to Love Your Husband His Way*. To sum up the importance of building intimacy:

> "Intimacy is a process, not an event, and it doesn't end with marriage. Find it and you've found the golden goose that will lay golden eggs forever."
>
> - Sean Platt
Simplemarriage.net

Link 3: Sex

> "Billions of people have had sex. I don't know how many have actually made love."

- Sheila Wray Gregoire
"To Love, Honor, Vacuum"

This is the third link in the chain because without romance and intimacy being strong in your marriage, your sex life will be anemic, at best.

I just did an Internet search on the word "sex," and it came back indicating that there were over 3 billion possible hits. I also searched "Christian sex," and it showed there were over 116 million possible connections.

A moment of transparency: I became addicted to sex (albeit, unhealthy sex) at the age of twelve from my first exposure to pornography. There is no doubt that for more than thirty years it warped my view of what Biblical marital sex should be. Even though I fought the addiction and worked hard at "making love" to my wife, rather than just having sex with her, it still impacted our love life for a long time.

I like what Dr. Wyatt Fisher says on this subject:

> "The sexual temperature within marriage, defined as the level of mutual sexual satisfaction, usually reflects the overall health of a marriage. If a marriage is healthy and connected, both partners typically report relatively frequent and fulfilling sex. However, if a marriage is unhealthy and disconnected, one or both partners usually report infrequent and unsatisfying sexual contact.
>
> "Sex is also usually one of the first things to enter a romantic relationship when things are going well and one of the first things to disappear when things turn south. Unfortunately, many men feel sexually unsatisfied in their marriages, while women tend to feel used just for their bodies. Obviously, learning how to have fulfilling Christian sex within marriage is essential."

- www.ChristianCrush.com
Article, "Christian Sex: Top 6 Steps to Fulfillment Within Marriage!"

I think the catchphrase here is "Obviously, learning how to have fulfilling Christian sex within marriage is essential."

I believe most men (like me) think we knew all we needed to before we ever started to try to make love to our wives. I now know that is sheer nonsense. First of all, note that I didn't say, "Have sex"; I said, "Make love." Any dog can have sex, but only humans can make love. I find it interesting that when I entered "Make Love" into the search engine it provided 135 million possible links, as opposed to the over 3 billion from the word "sex."

I have found very little written on making love from a Biblical worldview. There is one resource that both Cindy and I highly recommend for both the husband and wife to access if you want a crash course in "how to." It comes from the website To Love, Honor, and Vacuum. (Guys, don't get hung up on what the website is called.) Sheila Wray Gregoire has free resources as well as books written on this matter that you can purchase. She provides short chunks of great information that both men and women can get a lot out of.

I read through a few of these and found myself wishing this resource had been available to Cindy and me forty-six years ago. Things would have been a lot different—and a lot better.

What to Do When One of You Doesn't Want Sex

Men, there's one last aspect of this topic that I need to address, and that is withholding sex. There is a common misconception that all men want as much sex as they can get all the time. We know that's just not true.

While it doesn't happen as often with the husband withholding sex from his wife, it is happening more and more. We know because we hear from the wives who are really upset when it's happening to them.

WebMD lists the ten primary reasons husbands don't want, or will withhold, sex. They include taking antidepressants or other medications that can affect libido; sexual/porn addiction, masturbation; lack of sleep; hormonal issues (low testosterone); identity issues; relationship problems (i.e., arguing a lot); stress, etc. You could also have been the victim of sexual abuse as a child that can affect your desire for sex now.

Yes, all of these can be a problem and cause you to want to withhold sex from your wife. But as a Christian husband, we need to remember our call is to put our wife's needs ahead of our own. (See 1 Corinthians 7:3-5.) And it's not fair that she is deprived if you have a problem that can be resolved—either through medication or counseling, or both.

Cindy is writing about how she withheld sex from me for a number of years after we were first married because of what she suffered in her past.

Through therapy and God's healing, our physical relationship was made whole... until . . .

Having been a Type-1 diabetic for forty-four years, one of the side effects of the disease is impotence, which I've experienced for several years now. But in spite of my depleted libido and inability to achieve an erection, Cindy and I have found other creative ways to have an extremely satisfying sexual relationship in our mid-60s. Sure, I could have felt sorry for myself and "justified" withholding sexual intimacy. But I knew that would be wrong, as much as it was wrong when she withheld sex from me years ago.

It comes down to this simple maxim: when you have a problem, it becomes your wife's problem. If your wife has a problem, it becomes your problem. That's what the Bible calls to "bear one another's burdens." (Galatians 6:2 NIV) And when we do bear each other's burdens we fulfill the law of Christ.

My problem became Cindy's problem. But as partners in our marriage, we were committed to finding the solution. You need to be as committed to finding the solution necessary to keep your sexual relationship alive.

I want to add one more thing for clarity. Once I found out the reason for Cindy withholding sex from me (past sexual abuse), it changed my feeling from being a victim, too. God gave me compassion and the ability to extend grace to her as she went through the healing process she needed. So, if you and your wife are in a similar place right now, you need to be the hero and extend mercy and grace to your wife.

I started this chapter with the illustration of the three-link chain (Link 1 = Romance; Link 2 = Intimacy; and Link 3 = Sex). The husband holds one side of the chain and the wife the other. The strength of this chain is what will keep your marriage strong. It will take both of you committed to what Pastor John Piper says:

> "Jesus' teaching in general [implies] that happy and fulfilling sexual relations in marriage depend on each partner aiming to give satisfaction to the other. If it is the joy of each to make the other happy, a hundred problems will be solved before they happen."

As everyone knows, a chain is only as strong as its weakest link. Cindy's and my prayer is that your chain will remain strong as you each endeavor to make the other happy.

For additional reading on this issue, go to the Marriage Missions International website and read through the Topic, "Sexual Issues." A few examples are:

> What Do I Do When I Don't Want to Do It?... My Spouse Has Little or No Desire for Sex... Sexual Refusal: He Stopped Asking, but He Didn't Stop Wanting... Can't Have an Orgasm?... Sexual Attention Deficit Disorder... When Past Sexual Abuse Affects a Marriage's Intimacy... Battling Temptation with the Sword of Truth... Haunted by Premarital Sex... We Have Different Sex Drives... Haunted by Premarital Sex... SEX: When the Husband Doesn't Want to Make Love... and at least another dozen related articles on this subject.

Cindy

Invigorate or reinvigorate your romantic and sex life with each other. That marriage essential is easier said than done, but it is possible. It's like what author Fawn Weaver once said, "A great marriage isn't something that just happens; it's something that must be created."

Many married partners need to create a romantic and intimate life together. It is long gone. But hand-in-hand with God, all things are possible. Please don't forget that. For others, they need to rebuild. There may be some semblance of a love life still going on between them, but it's lacking. It needs extra doses of reinvigorating. And for other married couples, they need to continue to grow their romantic and sexual life together. They have a good foundation, and things are going well. But if it doesn't continue to grow forward, it will fall backward. And who wants that?

I'm not thinking most anyone would. That is evidenced by the articles that are visited the most on the Marriage Missions website. Sex and romance, in the context of marriage, are the issues that visitors are more interested in reading about. There is also the issue of adultery, which is a hot topic because many spouses are searching for solid Biblical help in that area.

The Intimacy of Romance (and Having Sex Together, Too)

However, at this point, I'd like to talk a bit about romance and sexual intimacy, within the context of marriage. They truly do go hand in hand. It's difficult to have one without the other. I'm not just talking about having sex together. Anyone can do that. Animals and insects can do that too. I'm talking about the deep intimacy that a husband and wife should have for each other within the context of expressing their sexuality in their marriage.

Unlike animals and insects, humans are one of the few species that actually can have sex face-to-face. It isn't until recently that I realized this. But it's an interesting point to consider. As I pondered this matter, I wondered—could it be that God gave us the ability to make love while facing each other for a purpose? I'm thinking so. I believe it's because experiencing oneness physically and emotionally, as a husband and wife, is extremely important. And it's difficult to achieve intimacy if you can't face each other during your most vulnerable times. When you make love, it is definitely one of those vulnerable times. Just being together one on one is a vulnerable time.

Concerning sexual times together it's true what author Tim Gardner wrote, "The goal of sex in marriage is the big O (and it ain't orgasm). It's oneness. Loving the whole person, not just the body parts." We'll talk more about that later, but first I'd like to talk about romance because it usually precedes the sexual relationship between a husband and wife. It helps to bring emotional "oneness" to the forefront in our relationship. When you do, sexual expression as marital partners is much more loving and unselfish. You care about each other at a deeper, giving level.

We already talked a bit about romance in the previous marriage essential. But I believe it needs to be expanded upon a bit more in this one. It's as we said the last time: you need to be intentional to grow your love relationship in deeper ways spiritually, emotionally, and sexually. But you also have to reinvigorate it from time to time. You need to shake it up; find ways to spice it up so you're both still loving each other and your life together. Just as with cooking, a little spice applied here and there can make a dish much more interesting. Add some spice to your romantic life with each other in the same way. Some of us need more spicing, and others not so much… but just do it. Do what it takes to grow this aspect of your relationship.

Most couples have some type of a romantic life going on between them before they marry. After all, why would they even think of marrying in the first place? Something loving and romantic was most likely going on before they married. Something intrigued them to want to continue getting to know each other. And from there, they decided that this was "the one" they wanted to spend the rest of their lives living within marital partnership.

Going Past the Original Bonding Time

It only goes to reason that if romance was there in the original bonding time before you married, the romantic relationship needs to continue on into the marriage relationship. You don't fill a car's gas tank up one time with fuel, or even a whole lot of times in the beginning, and then expect everything to keep running smoothly without any refills. Eventually, everything stops running, and the ride is over. It's the same way in marriage. You have to keep filling up each other's marital "love tank," so to speak.

Please don't let your love dry out in your marriage. But if it has—whether it's just that your romantic life is flat together, or if it's like the "check engine" light is giving you a warning, or it has already sputtered where you don't see much life in it at all, do something about that. Each day can bring a new beginning if you look at it that way. Start again in romancing the one who you vowed to love for the rest of your life. Don't just say you will—let your words push forth into truth in words, and action.

Romance is not just going out on date nights and such, although to most spouses (especially wives), this is important too. That's one of the reasons we have a whole topic dedicated to "Romantic Ideas." Most every article is packed with reasons to date and different date ideas for married couples. Several of the articles take you to other websites to read some of their dating ideas too. As we get further along in marriage, we need all the help we can get. We can get lulled into thinking, "We've been there, and done that, too," because we gain a longer history together.

But please know that we keep adding more and more ideas and links to the articles posted, so keep visiting that topic. And if you've used up the ideas we have posted, and you need more, and don't see any, just let us know. It will spur us on to post additional ones that we can find. We'd love it if you can share with us some of your ideas, as well.

Many Splendid Benefits

I agree with something Gary Thomas wrote in the article (posted on his website) titled, "The Many Quiet but Splendid Benefits of Marriage." I even like the title, because even quiet little things we do for each other can heighten the romantic feelings we have for each other. And, indeed, they can be splendid. Gary writes:

> "So often we hope marriage keeps serving up those endless and inexhaustible moments of 'special romance,' whirlwind feelings, 'carry me away' moments. But, in reality, sometimes marriage is built on small things, quiet but splendid benefits, like having someone find your cell phone when you're tired of looking for it yourself."

Gary is referring to an incident that happened in his marriage. Steve and I have others that come to mind, such as one spouse finding the other's lost glasses or an important paper, or washing, or filling up with gas the other's car, and not saying a word. I'm sure you have some of your own when you think about it.

You need to truly grow an intimate relationship beyond "just" having sex. Sure, having sex together brings a wonderful high. I'm not criticizing it. I love it, and am all for it. But again, you need to be intimate with each other in many different ways.

Romance also involves flirting with each other and spending time laughing together. We too often forget to do that after we get married. We've heard it said that life multiplies in its busyness the longer we are married (at least in the earlier years). We believe that is true. We've lived it and seen it happen in marriages all around us. That's why we need to be intentional in looking for ways to romance each other, even in little ways.

> "Wise husbands and wives need to take time to practice small acts of touching. Hold hands in a walk through the mall. Stopping to rub your mate's shoulders for a moment. Take the time to gently hold your spouse at the door on your way out. These small but important acts can work like 'super-bloom' to a plant and green out a relationship."
>
> - Gary Smalley

Steve and I love to flirt with each other. We usually try to do it so no one else sees these romantic little gestures. Sometimes it's a fluttering of the eyes, a wink, or brushing up against each other. It could be that we blow a kiss or give a little smile that says without words, "I'm loving you." I don't know if you did this with each other before you got married. If you did, don't stop. Keep flirting with your spouse. If you stopped, then start again. You may just give your spouse a quick jump-start for his or her heart that will warm things up between the two of you. Don't let familiarity kill your marriage relationship. Use it to speak in loving ways that no one else on earth will understand but you and your spouse.

Steve and I often talk of our history together. We laugh over things we've done in the past and things our kids, grandkids, family, and friends have done. Just saying a word or two, and we both start laughing because we know what the other spouse is referring to that no one else would understand. It's like a private light turns on, just between the two of us, and the laughter connects us in an endearing way. That is one of those "splendid benefits" of being married—especially someone you've been married to for a long time. It's the type of "oneness" experiences we need to grow in our marriages.

Steve and I believe it's important to be playful with each other. It's important to flirt, tease (in an honoring way), and build fun memories together. Simone Signoret said something we believe to be true, "Chains do not hold a marriage together. It is threads, hundreds of tiny threads, which sew people together through the years." Some of the threads we sew are done through the infusion of genuine laughter over shared moments together.

There is a game we play with each other. It's one of those threads we keep sewing. I call it the "hide the little rhino" game. It started probably nine or so years ago. Steve found a miniature gray rhino knickknack somewhere. It's about the size of a walnut. He showed it to me and I suggested he just pitch it. Instead, I found that he put it on my dresser. I thought to myself, "Why would he put it there?" So, I returned the "favor" and put it on his dresser. The next thing I knew I found it in my jewelry box. I put it into a box he had, and that's when the "game" began. It has been placed back and forth over the years ever since, going from this place to that—wherever we think the other will find it and have to deal with it.

Do you know that all these years Steve and I never talk about this? It has been a quirky little game we lovingly play with each other, and yet we never discuss it. But I'll tell you, every time I see that little rhino, it brings a little giggle to my heart. It's like an "I love playing this funny little game with you" type of thing that until now, no one but Steve and I have known about. And even though Steve will read this and see what I just wrote, we still won't talk about it... will we, Steve? (I'm thinking that at this point he will say, "Nope!") So, let the games continue!

Hopefully, you're working on building good memories that will help you so the more difficult ones step back a bit further into the background of your memory bank. Even silly memories can cause this to happen. These memories help to take the sting out of those difficult situations.

Infusing Humor into Your Relationship Is Important

Steve and I strongly believe that humor is one of the most important things that we need to KEEP alive and healthy within the marriage. We are always on the lookout to find ways to laugh together. It brings us closer together. Laughter is one of the first things that leaves a marriage that needs reinvigorating. It's easy to take life (and each other) too seriously. We forget to laugh together as we did before we got married.

"Wise experts agree that the best way for anyone to cope is with a good laugh. 'Humor makes all things tolerable,' said preacher Henry Ward Beecher. 'Laugh out loud,' says Chuck Swindoll. 'It helps flush out the nervous system.' On another occasion, Chuck said, 'Laughter is the most beautiful and beneficial therapy God ever granted humanity.' Arnold Glasgow said, 'Laughter is a tranquilizer with no side effects.'

> "The point is that even when you've had a tough day, or should we say especially when you've had a tough day, you need to laugh. It will help wash away the stress and keep the two of you together. So help each other to find something funny even when it's not easy."
>
> - Drs. Les and Leslie Parrott
> "The Love List"

I remember a number of years ago we had a lot of very serious issues going on in our lives. We were dealing with life-and-death situations and all kinds of complicating matters. There didn't seem to be much to laugh about. It was as if all of the joy had drained out of our home. But one day it occurred to us that we just couldn't allow life to keep punching at us like that. We needed to put up some type of a fight—a fight to find ways to laugh together. It wouldn't change the situations, but we knew it could help to change our attitudes towards them and each other. We were starting to nitpick at each other (which we knew would lead to more serious fighting). It was important to level things out a bit. We both came to realize that we needed that.

We made it our mission to look for ways to laugh together. And when we purposefully looked, we found them, and it helped more than I can tell you. We also grew closer to each other as well, because we weathered another storm and came out of it stronger.

Through the years, we sometimes watch a funny movie. Or we invite friends over for a game night. We make it a rule that no serious stuff is to be discussed during that time together. Sometimes we read funny comic strips together, such as Far Side, Calvin and Hobbs, Baby Blues, Herman, or something else humorous. We've even gone onto Youtube and have watched funny things there, starting with one funny clip and then go on from there. The point isn't what we've done, but that we did it together, with the intention of infusing laughter back into our relationship.

Putting laughter into our marriage has been a great mission because "a cheerful heart is as good medicine" as the Bible tells us (Proverbs 17:22, NIV). We recommend you multiply times of laughter into your marriage. We have quite a bit on this subject posted on the Marriage Missions website. And most of the blogs and articles have some fun things in them, with jokes and videos that are humorous. Just put the word "laugh" into the search feature, and I think you'll be pleased.

Going Back to Basics

Infusing laughter into your marriage is a way to reinvigorate your romantic life together. But so is going back to what helped you fall in love with each other in the first place. I love the marriage tip that Patrick and Dwaina Six (from Marriages.net) gave on this topic:

> "Recently we saw an article produced by Focus on the Family featuring a couple who, after 13 years of marriage, noticed their fire diminishing into embers. They had a great idea. They decided to start acting like teenagers—starry-eyed crazy for one another. They began to plan secret get-aways. They began to touch each other again, to look deep into one another's eyes again. Do you know what? The passion returned! We can learn a valuable lesson from teens in love. Together, begin to develop a new mindset that says, 'I just

want to be alone with you.' 'When will I see you again?' 'I can't wait.'"

This idea really works. We've done this, and we've seen many, many others do the same thing, and it has helped them. It kind of reminds me of the incident I heard about a while back about something football coach Vince Lombardi said to his team. They were sitting in the locker room after a crushing defeat. Frustrated, Vince looked at them and decided they needed to go back to the basics in football. They had been messing up all over the place with little mistakes they made here and there. These are basic mistakes that helped them to lose the football game. Vince looked at them, held up a football, and said, "Guys, this is a football. I want to take you back to the basics because you've obviously forgotten them."

It's the same with us sometimes in marriage. If we're forgetting to romance each other and are treating each other as enemies, rather than lovers, we need to get back to the basics. Bring back to mind the things we did together that helped us fall in love with each other in the first place. And throw in some added romantic gestures, as well.

Here are two quick tips back-to-back that might help you to do just that:

> "Reintroduce the element of surprise. Identify patterns and break routines. Become unpredictable. Celebrate anything and everything. Buy the unexpected present. Take an unplanned trip."
>
> - Jim Magruder
> www.todayschristianwoman.com
> Article, "4 Ways to Rekindle Intimacy"

We have other suggestions posted in the Romantic Ideas topic of our website. Just look around.

> "Starting right now, do something for your husband or wife that they wouldn't expect. If you aren't accustomed to it, vacuum the floor or do the dishes without having to be asked. Turn off the television, look at your spouse and begin talking. Then, do it again tomorrow! Start to do things that show your love. Adjust your behavior daily to express how much you love your spouse and enjoy the changes after that."
>
> - Dr. Randy Carlson

Stretch Yourselves on This One

Now guys, do your best to stretch yourself on this. Yes, it could be that you aren't the most romantic guy on the planet. And you may be tired much of the time too. But don't let that stop you from finding little ways, and hopefully big ones, to romance your bride and reinvigorate your romantic life with your wife.

And gals, give grace here. Don't expect him to be the one to plan everything. Yes, there are probably many of you who are reading this who can testify that you're the one who does all the romancing. If you aren't happy about this, I'm truly sorry that you find yourself in this place. In a perfect world, it wouldn't be. But we don't live in a perfect world. Even though your husband should do a lot of the romancing, deal with reality, rather than piling your expectations higher than it's realistic to do so. Be the one in the marriage who initiates the romantic times. What's the big deal?

I love the following quote by author Melanie Chitwood. It helped me to get a handle on reality, and it has helped many, many other women do the same. She wrote:

> "Instead of waiting for your husband to be romantic, go ahead and try initiating romance yourself. That's right—you! Sometimes we women cling to the silly notion that spelling it out for husbands ruins the romance. We want our husbands to read our minds and create the romantic evening we've always dreamed of. Well, frankly, we need to get over it! If we don't invest the romantic love, we take the risk that our marriage will become dull, boring, and disconnected. More marriages die because two people drift apart than because of a crisis, such as infidelity.
>
> ". . . Maybe your husband's idea of romance looks a little different from yours. Maybe he's deathly afraid of being vulnerable and looking like a fool by being romantic. Maybe you'll have to build up his confidence and be creative to resurrect romantic love, but the results will be worth the effort!"

- Melanie Chitwood
"What a Husband Needs from His Wife"

That really freed up my thinking in this area of married life, and others, as well. Too often we let the world shove at us these idealisms, wrapped up in falsities that can cause us to be unhappy with our own situations. We've got to stop allowing them to do that. Hollywood, television shows, and romance novels (to name a few) are taking us hostage in warping our thinking, when we let them.

I'm not saying that you shouldn't try to get your spouse to participate with you in the romance part of your marriage. I'm just saying, be careful that you don't allow fantasies and imaginations to be fed within our minds to the point where they sabotage our marriages. Look, seek, and find new ideas. They're out there. But don't go crazy about it. Relax and enjoy "The many quiet but splendid benefits of marriage" too. Infuse, reinvigorate, but also relax in just knowing that out of all of the people in the world, your spouse chose you to love, and you chose him or her. ENJOY!

Romance Leads to Sexual Intimacy Too

I'd like to talk about the issue of sex within marriage. I'm going to begin with the basics of sexual intimacy between husbands and wives. And then I'll go into more complicating issues that divide marital partners.

First, I feel compelled to say that I agree with the point Gary Chapman makes on the purpose of sex. He writes:

> "What is the purpose of sex in marriage? What was God's design? Scripture clearly reveals three reasons. The first, and most obvious, is procreation. It was God's design to provide a safe haven in which to rear children. A second purpose is to provide companionship. Sex is designed to be a bonding experience. The biblical concept is 'They will become one flesh' (Genesis 2:24, NIV). The idea is deep companionship, which is why it's reserved for marriage. A third purpose for sex in marriage is pleasure. If you doubt this, read the Song of Songs."
>
> - www.Lifeway.com
> Article, "True Intimacy in Marriage"

That's so true! All three points are important to remember—safety, companionship, and pleasure. It does seem that God created marital sex for all three purposes.

Safety, Companionship, and Pleasure

Within the sanctity of marriage, God wants us to enjoy safety. It is supposed to be a "safe haven" for our children and for us too. You build trust with each other, which brings a sense of security. We are to share intimate moments with each other in ways that we share them with no one else. That makes our relationship all the more intimate.

The Hebrew word for sexual intercourse is the term "to know." God designed this physical act to be a way that we come "to know" each other in a way that we are not "to know" anyone else. We are to be a safe place for our spouse to be with—trusting that there is safety built into our being together as husband and wife in all aspects of our marriage.

> "Make it your goal to create a marriage that feels like it is the safest place on earth."
>
> - Gary Smalley

There is also COMPANIONSHIP. This can draw you closer together physically, as well as emotionally. There is "oneness" and bonding that is to be truly unique. You feel comfortable being with and doing things for your marriage partner in a way that draws you closer together again. You are part of a couple—no longer alone.

But we need to remember, "Companionship time involves much more than simply being in the same place at the same time" (Glenn Wagner). It takes involvement together. You need to be present emotionally and physically for intimacy companionship to truly happen.

And then there is the one that is most emphasized in today's world, pleasure. If both partners are being unselfish in their lovemaking, if they give and receive—there is pleasure beyond description.

Gary Chapman also proposes that "you make a list of suggestions you'd like to give to your spouse that would make marriage intimacy better for you."

I thought about that. I wondered what I would put on my list for Steve. After forty-six plus years of marriage, there isn't much more that I could imagine that I could add. But I did think of a few things (private to everyone else but Steve and me). Perhaps you can think of a few for your spouse that you would put on that list. And it would be good to have your spouse do the same thing—make a list for you. It's a bold move. But intimacy includes bold moves within the safety of a loving, marital relationship.

Sexual Dysfunction and Tension

Now, what if there is sexual dysfunction going on within the marriage? It could be acted out from the actions of the wife, or it could come from the actions of the husband. Or perhaps there is tension because both of you are not being generous with each other in your marital bed. You are in conflict because of on-going selfish actions—making your marital bed into a war zone.

I feel a need to say this first. I'll address the guys first. Guys, I don't know how to emphasize enough. Most wives will not be the least interested in making love to you if they don't feel loved by you. There are exceptions. But we hear from wives over and over and over again that they are tired and feel taken advantage of by their husbands. If their husbands would help them more, and even initiate picking up the load of work that needs to be done before going to bed at night, it would be received as foreplay. That's not exclusively why you do that because wives can see through those actions too. It can be one reason, but it should not be the only reason.

Yeah, it didn't use to be that way. Years ago (and in some countries) the wife did all of the work at home, and the husband worked outside of the home. And it could appear that it was only fair for the wives to do all of the domestic work, and be the one to nurture and take care of the children. That was recognized as her vital contribution to the family. And husbands gave their all to make sure that their wives and children were well cared for financially. That was his contribution to the family. And then when it came to the bedroom, when the husband wanted it, it was recognized that it was his right to demand it. The wife had less say in all of this matter.

But things have and are changing in our world. In some homes and cultures, it is still that way. What I say about this is that if it works for them, then great! There is no problem. But if it doesn't work in your marriage, it's important to work with reality. We need to work more with how things are rather than how they used to be or how we think they should be. (Of course, when it flies in the face of Biblical truth—that is entirely different. But this is one of those gray areas, rather than a black-and-white one—a truth versus opinion situation.)

In today's world, we have wives who say their husband's only help out when they want something sexual from them. Men, please check your motives and your actions on this. If you're only helping out with the kids or housework (or almost always) only when you want your wife to make love, she is most likely going to feel used and will feel resentful. She needs partnership in dealing with the busy matters that keep your home and your children doing well. It gets exhausting to try to juggle it all with little or no help.

Plus, she needs romancing and intimate conversations with you. Having meaningful conversations (beyond just reporting information that has or will occur) with you means as much to her as sexual touch means to you. It's your differing ways of feeling intimately connected.

Think about it, though. It's only reasonable that you get involved in caring for the home and the family. She isn't your servant; she is your wife. Household responsibilities, along with taking care of the children God gave to both of you, should be shared by both spouses. This is especially true if both of you are working other jobs as well.

And it's also reasonable that spouses should talk together in deep, meaningful ways. Otherwise, your wife feels alone within your marital partnership. And we know what God says about men (and women) being alone: "It is not good." You were created to address a particular type of aloneness that a marital relationship should fill. It's all about growing your relationship with God and with your spouse. Both are important to maintain and grow.

Do you truly believe this is how Jesus would have you treat your bride? Do you believe He would tell you to only help around the house and with the kids when you want your wife to be sexually active with you? And do you believe Jesus would have you only connect in conversation and being together with your bride when you want to connect sexually? I don't; we don't. Again, look at the context of 1 Corinthians 7, and you will see that when you marry, your spouse is to be your first human priority. That includes all areas of making your life work together.

Be Considerate of Each Other's Sexual Needs

And gals, please be considerate of your husband's needs in this area of marriage (just as he should be considerate of yours). We have husbands who write to us at Marriage Missions who tell us they are working full time, and their wives are at home (or are working part-time). And yet their wives expect their husbands to pick up the same workload of maintaining their home (sometimes more) as them. And she is home many more hours of the day to do this than he is.

He does all of this, and then she continually tells him she's too tired to make love. And I'm not just talking about a few times here and there. One excuse is given after another. Sometimes the wife is "too tired" or she isn't interested in making love, etc. And that is fine sometimes. We all have our "off" days. (I'll talk more about this later.) But it's problematic when the sexual refusals continue throughout the year (sometimes, not even making love one time a year, or just a few times, at best). Truly, this just isn't healthy for the relationship unless they both are in agreement with this arrangement.

There's a "joke" going around that tells a lot concerning this issue (although it is not a "ha-ha" funny joke):

> "A therapist has a theory that couples who make love once a day are the happiest. So he tests it at a seminar by asking those assembled, 'How many people here make love once a day?' Half the people raise their hands, each of them grinning widely. 'Once a week?' A third of the audience members raise their hands, their grins a bit less vibrant. 'Once a month?' A few hands tepidly go up. Then he asks, 'OK, how about once a year?'
>
> "One man in the back jumps up and down, jubilantly waving his hands. The therapist is shocked—this disproves his theory. 'If you make love only once a year,' he asks, 'why are you so happy?' The man yells, 'Today's the day!'"

- As posted on www.Rd.com

We can chuckle at the absurdity of this joke. But for the spouse (acknowledging that sometimes it's the wife) who lives in this type of marital existence, this is definitely no joking matter. What's really sad is that this happens in more homes than most people realize! This is not what God expects of us, especially when He tells us to "love one another in word and deed." It also goes against what we're told in the Bible:

> "The husband should give to his wife her conjugal rights, and likewise the wife to her husband. For the wife does not have authority over her own body, but the husband does. Likewise, the husband does not have authority over his own body, but the wife does. Do not deprive one another, except perhaps by agreement for a limited time, that you may devote yourselves to prayer; but then come together again, so that Satan may not tempt you because of your lack of self-control."
>
> - 1 Corinthians 7:3-5
> ESV

If you are continually pushing your marriage partner away from you sexually, when he or she desires you, please know that it's almost as if your spouse is being shoved into a sexual hostage situation at that point. It's a sin for him or her to have sex with anyone else. So where is he or she to go for release, concerning his or her sexual urges? They don't just go away because you or your spouse wants them to vanish. We don't live in a pretend world. We must deal with reality. If we don't, all kinds of unhealthy, unloving situations can develop and cause problems for the marriage. We give the enemy of our faith a blank check to cash in on tempting the spouse who is left wanting sexual intimacy. By depriving our spouse of sexual intimacy, it shoves our marital partner into the direction of exposure to greater outside temptations.

This can be equated with something marital expert Michelle Weiner-Davis points out:

> "Many spouses with lower sex drives are essentially saying, 'I know you're sexually unhappy. I won't do anything about that, but I still expect you to remain faithful.' Can you see what's wrong with this picture?"
>
> - Christianity Today, August 2003
> Article, "When Your Sex Drives Don't Match"

There *is* something wrong with this picture! The sexual relationship is an important part of being married. God acknowledges that in the Bible. As a result, so should we. If it weren't important, those scriptures wouldn't be as strongly stated as they are. There's no guessing what God feels about us depriving each other in that way.

If neither of you feels deprived, then that's great! But if one of you does, then you both have a problem that you need to work through so you both are in agreement.

If you "aren't interested," then make it a mission to find a way to become interested. It can happen. I know; it has happened to me at times (and it happens to other women, who have told me the same thing concerning their sexual situations). So, I'm going to confess something here. There have been times when I have not been "interested" in being sexually active with my husband. I have a lower sex drive than Steve does. But we have both learned to stretch ourselves in this area of our life together. Steve is more compassionate in not asking as much as he might have otherwise. And I am more responsive in being more sexually active with him than I would be otherwise. Over the years we have learned to give and take so we are both satisfied.

So, this is what I have done on different occasions when I am not "in the mood" but Steve is. When Steve approaches me to make love, and I'm not as interested, I start (silently) praying. I ask God to give me the desire to meet his needs. I'm sure this seems weird to some, but it works. Steve isn't even aware that I am doing this. But as I pray and lean my thoughts in that direction, eventually, I find myself desiring my husband to the same degree that he desires intimacy.

There are times when it takes a bit longer to line my desires up with my actions. So, I start to get involved in making love to him as a generous lover before I'm even truly interested. I'm sure this doesn't make sense to some of you who are reading this. My main desire is to give him pleasure as his wife. But something happens along the way. As I pray and get involved in my mind, and my body responds towards Steve, my emotions and desires start to line up with my actions. I start out to please him, but eventually, I'm completely involved, and I end up loving every moment of it as much as he does. It truly is amazing!

Yes, there are times where one of you wants to make love and the other really can't. One of you is sick, or under the weather, or is tired, or out of sorts. That happens. In those incidences, the "wanting" spouse should give grace and space when that happens. If that's the case, then the denying spouse should look for another time soon afterward to sexually approach the other spouse. But make the denials more of the exception, rather than the rule, if it's at all possible.

If it's because of time issues, physical problems, emotional and/or abuse issues, lower sex drive, mismatched sex drives, hygiene matters, or whatever... make it your mission to work on that area of your life together.

On this issue, Paul and Lori Byerly, from The Marriage Bed website make a good point:

> "Some spouses seem to have a never-ending supply of 'good reasons' for saying no. None of the reasons seems unfair. But taken as a whole it's obvious something is wrong. When a constant stream of reasons for not having sex continues for very long, there is some underlying reason for the lack of sex. The reasons given are merely convenient. Or they could be concocted excuses that hide the real problem. The truth is that we make time and energy for the things, which are most important to us. So when we are routinely too busy or too tired for something it suggests that the real issue is more about priorities than time."
>
> - site.themarriagebed.com
> Article, "My Spouse Won't Have Sex"

Keep in mind what one of the biggest goals is of marriage. It is oneness. Jesus emphasized the unique "oneness" of marriage. In Matthew 19:4-6 (ESV) of the Bible, Jesus is recorded in saying,

> "Have you not read that he who created them from the beginning made them male and female, and said, 'Therefore a man shall leave his father and his mother and hold fast to his wife, and the two shall become one flesh'? So they are no longer two but one flesh. What therefore God has joined together let no man separate."

You can't be "one" in flesh if you are denying yourself sexually to your other half when he or she is repeatedly left wanting. Your spouse is the one you are to cleave to, as God ordains. Keep in mind—whether you are the husband or the wife—something that Tim Gardner wrote:

> "The goal of sex is the big O (and it ain't orgasm). It's ONENESS. Loving the whole person, not just the body parts."

Did you get that? Yes, body parts are often emphasized, but "oneness" goes beyond these body parts. It involves give and take, and being unselfish and generous sexually.

That brings up another important aspect of being generous sexually. It's another sexual situation that happens many times in marriages. In some marriages, a wife does "give in" to have "sex" with her husband. But she lets him know in different ways that she feels bothered by the whole situation. It's quite apparent to the husband that he is not making love to his wife; he is having sex with an uninterested wife who just wants him to "hurry up and get it over with."

There is nothing loving about treating your marriage partner in this way. This is wrong if it is the wife who acts in this manner, or if it's the husband who acts in this way. It is unkind, dishonoring, and totally unloving to act this way towards a spouse you promised to "love and honor" for the rest of your life. If you're having trouble with the feeling of oneness in your intimate life together, you may need to get help. It could be through a counselor, books, prayer, talking together, etc.... but please make it your mission not to make your bedroom a war zone. If one of you is dissatisfied, then both of you are affected. And both of you need to do your part to make this a non-issue. You are married partners, not married singles. Get help so this does not cause division between you! Show love as God would have you.

It's like something I heard the other day, "We love because He first loved us." Let's be generous with our love for each other in every aspect of love that is presented to us within our marriages.

Past Sexual Abuse

I want to make another point about this intimacy issue. It's an important one that I pray will make a major difference. Past sexual abuse is one of the reasons many wives and husbands (yes, this happens to guys too) deny the other sexually. I want to emphasize this because it is one I dealt with, and more women than I can count talk to me about this being a problem for them as well. Many, many, many wives deal with this horrible issue... although, sometimes it is the husband who was abused sexually in the past. But moreover, I have wives who tell me directly (or post on the Marriage Missions website) that they sexually withhold from their spouse because of past abuse.

I confess that I am a wife who was abused sexually by two different male relatives earlier in my life. Both of them (and their wives) are now deceased. So at this point, I feel at liberty to talk openly about how it adversely affected my life and my marriage. I have posted a few articles on our website, so I feel no compulsion to repeat it here. If you want to learn more about my journey of recovery in this, please go to the "Sexual Issues" part of our website to read about it there.

I will also talk more about this in one of the other essentials we will be giving. But within this essential, from my experience, I need to say that I know how horribly one's past abuse can haunt a spouse for years. I have lived through this. And sadly, I allowed it to also haunt Steve because I passed my victimhood onto him and denied him sexually because of my pain more times than either of us cares to remember. Steve was, for the most part, very understanding and patient about all of this during those difficult times as I healed and recovered from it.

The reason I'm sad about this is because I allowed it to go on for way too long. I should have gotten help a lot sooner than I did. I justified it in my mind that because of what happened to me, Steve should be compassionate and not pressure me in that way. And that is true to a certain extent, but I took it too far. I let my victimization shut me down so our intimate times became battlefields, instead of endearing times. I needed to get help so I could be released from my prison of pain. The bonus is that at that point Steve would no longer be an additional victim of those men who hurt me.

I projected their wicked actions onto Steve. I recoiled from many of his romantic advances, and I made him feel like a bad person for wanting me sexually. As I look back, I see that he wanted me sexually, but he also wanted the "oneness" that this type of intimacy could bring to our marriage. I expected him to stay faithful to me, but I didn't want to satisfy his needs and wants—only mine. (This is much like what I described earlier in this marriage essential.) This was selfish on my part. Why should I give those men any additional victories? I didn't deserve what happened to me. But Steve didn't deserve to be an additional victim either because of it. I needed to get some help, and I should have done it sooner than I did. We both lost out. I added pain on top of my pain, and pushed it onto my husband too.

Thankfully, God opened my eyes. Sadly, it was quite a few years into our marriage that this revelation came. (Guys and gals, I pray this gives you hope that even at later dates, those "ah-ha" moments can come.) I finally received the help I needed, and to this day I am continuing on my journey to healthy thinking and living. Steve and I are now closer than I could ever describe because of this. Now we deal with "normal" issues, rather than the toxic ones. And we deal with those in much healthier ways.

I say all of this to encourage spouses who have been abused to please properly deal with abuse matters. By closing your eyes to it, it won't go away. You have to deal with them in the ways that are most effective for you to get to a healthy place emotionally and physically. Please don't ignore, belittle, criticize, or dismiss your spouse's needs. They are legitimate to him or her, just as your needs are legitimate to you. On one of his television shows, I once heard Dr. Phil McGraw say something I totally agree with, concerning this issue:

> "Consider your partner's needs as legitimate, and look at how you can meet those needs. Don't label your partner as being wrong or having something wrong with him/her because that dismisses the issue."

Dismissing your spouse is not something that a marriage partner should ever do. His or her feelings are just as legitimate as yours. Different is not wrong; it's just different.

And if you are the spouse of someone who has been abused, please pray for your spouse and for yourself. Do what you can to stay pure, despite the temptation to be with others in ways you shouldn't. Don't allow yourself to believe the lie that because you hurt so badly, and are being denied, you have the right to cheat and fulfill your needs outside of the marriage covenant: that is a lie and is NOT acceptable. It is an integrity issue that you must maintain at all costs by trusting in God's strength to keep you. Even if your spouse is not doing what he or she should, it does not give you a license to do what is wrong, as a result.

Busyness

Enough said about abuse. There is more that needs to be said about sexual issues between a husband and wife than we will address in this format. But instead, I refer you to the "Sexual Issues" topic on our website so you can read learn more. There is also the "Pornography and Cybersex" topic that you may need to check out if this is the insidious problem you are dealing with in your marriage.

Plus, please know that we understand that there are some sexual issues that don't line up with what I just wrote. I get that, and so does Steve. There are some spouses who are totally selfish, narcissistic, and don't want to partner with their spouse, or are clueless in how they should. But please pray, read, and glean through all the info provided—both here and on our website, and then apply what you can use.

However, I want to quickly touch on one last point concerning your romantic and sexual life with each other, and that is busyness. Busyness can be a huge romantic killer. This has been another big factor in our marriage that inhibited the growth of our romantic life together over the years. We were so busy that we would fall into bed exhausted over and over again. This became problematic.

But it wasn't just problematic in our marriage; it is troublesome in a growing number of today's marriages. In doing research for their book, "The Gift of Sex," Cliff and Joyce Penner talked with several thousand people. Seventy-five percent of them said that lack of time was the greatest problem they were experiencing in their sex life. We've heard of statistics from other sources that back that up as well.

Raising kids especially brings this to the forefront. Here's a truth from Murphy's Law: "Sex makes little kids. Kids make little sex." The very act that brought the kids into your life in the first place is the very act that is often pushed aside when you have those kids. We have several articles (and links to additional ones) posted in the topic "Children's Effects on Marriage" on our website. Please read what we make available. You could find it helpful.

But also remember that this is a season of your life. You will have more time eventually. We've seen this to be true in our own lives. But for now, however, steal pockets of time whenever you can. Keep in mind something Dave Willis said:

> "Don't put your marriage on hold while you're raising your kids, or else you'll end up with an empty nest and an empty marriage."

That's so true. Children are loud and demanding, and your marriage may not be (or it doesn't seem like it is). But, actually, it is. It's just that marriage relationships have more of a tendency to go the way of a slow death caused by neglect.

Make your marriage a priority. Don't allow that which screams the loudest to take control of too much of your time and energy. Don't allow your lives to be so child-centered that you neglect each other. Yes, kids have valid needs that you need to meet. But it's also good for them to have a mom and dad who feed their romantic and sexual relationship with each other. It helps to preserve the marriage that they depend upon so that it remains intact and provides stability for the entire family. Do this for the sake of your marriage and for your children's security. They need a safe place to fall, and you want to make sure that both Mom and Dad are there for them in your home so that can happen. Growing a healthy marriage makes that possible.

Plus, kids need to learn to share in many different ways, and this is one of them. It's okay for them to be left wanting your company sometimes. If they get everything they want, when they want it, it can cause them to feel entitled to expect more than they should.

You are showing more love to your children when you show each other more love, as you promised you would do in your wedding vows. Make time to be together by shoving aside some of the less important things, so you have the time you need to nurture your marriage relationship.

Ask God to show you ways, big and small, that can help you find pockets of time (plus more at other times), so you can express your love to each other romantically and sexually. I read something written by Bill and Pam Farrell that could give you an idea you can use. They wrote:

> "When things got crazy, we would call a time-out and head to a hotel for 48 hours. We would have a private marriage conference. Just order room service and have sex and relax."
>
> - Bill and Pam Farrel
> "Red Hot Monogamy"

Of course, you'd have to fit this into your schedule somehow and your budget, but it's well worth it. I heard a commentator talking about this type of hotel visit the other day. He said that even if it were only for a few hours, it would be worth the time. It would cost about the same as a therapy session, but it would be a "whole lot more fun." Plus, you would have some great memories and be more energized to plow back into life. Think about it.

Creativity in Lovemaking

I want to make one last point on this topic of romance and sexuality. There are certain cases where one spouse or the other cannot "perform" in normal sexual ways. There are a whole host of reasons, from medical reasons (such as Diabetes, heart conditions, complications from accidents, pain issue, etc.) to medication complications, to age-related issues, etc. The list goes on. It's amazing that you don't hear much about this in the media and movie industry. They talk about what is "normal," but then you are left wondering what to do when you or your spouse doesn't fit in with their "perfect" sexual standard.

I don't know if you or your spouse fits into this category. If you do, seek medical help. Many times it's a switch of medications or a testosterone problem that can be dealt with medicinally. Sometimes things can be done, and other times nothing else can be done. You need to find out if this is the case; if you or your spouse is feeling stressed by this.

But if nothing can be done, and you can't make love in the "traditional" way, don't let that stop you. Be more creative in meeting each other's needs. Throw it out of your head that you can't be sexual if penetration is not possible. Be creative... experiment and find other ways to make love. If neither of you wants to make love, then that is fine. You don't have to make love in this way. Just make sure you grow your intimacy with each other in other ways, even if for valid reasons you have to take the sex act out of it. But if either of you are unhappy, look for ways to bring mutual satisfaction. The important thing is that you experience oneness in the ways that work for both of you. God blesses you all the more when you embrace each other in oneness.

> "As you reflect on the last year, how can you love and serve your spouse in sexual intimacy? How can you make sex a priority in your marriage? Think about it! Sex will bind you in a way that nothing else can! Trust God's plan in that."
>
> - Kate
> www.onefleshmarriage.com

Marriage Essential #4
Guard Your Heart, Mind, and Your Marriage

How important is it to guard your heart, mind, and marriage? We have hundreds of testimonies posted on our website from men (and women) whose marriages were destroyed because one of them didn't take this marriage essential seriously. We hope what we share will strengthen your personal resolve to: Guard Your Heart, Mind, and Marriage.

Cindy

In the previous marriage essentials, we've written about the importance of building a solid Biblical foundation in your marriage. Then we talked about growing your love relationship. But to build and to grow, it will take intentionality on your part. Love doesn't grow without participating in making that happen.

And then last time we talked about invigorating your romance and sex life with each other. They go hand-in-hand in many ways.

So now we are focusing on the importance of guarding your heart, your mind, and your marriage. This is another area of marriage where it also takes intentionality to make it happen. Otherwise, you are leaving yourself open to "chance." And we know where that can take us. Oh, if I only had a dollar for every time I have heard the phrase, "We didn't mean to fall in love; it just happened."

No, it didn't. It happened because spouses didn't guard their hearts, minds, or marriages. And when they felt a spark (which isn't an unusual occurrence) towards someone other than their spouse, they continued to walk towards it, rather than flee from it.

True love isn't something you fall into. You have to push it to make it grow to the point of being real. Infatuation takes no push. It is a type of infant "love" you can fall into in an instant. It involves tingles and imaginations and biochemicals flowing all over the place. And it's fun. There's no doubt about it. This is what drew us to our spouse in the first place. But if you don't grow it (especially before the newness wears off), and you don't guard what you have, your relationship can get to a shaky place because of neglect. And that is a dangerous place to be. We are more prone to do stupid things when we find ourselves in that type of situation.

Beware of False Love Appearing Real

Whatever you do, don't walk into the trap of falling in love with falling in love. That is like chasing rainbows. Some people are addicted to the feeling and process of "falling in love." It's an addictive high that they continually crave to experience. It's actually a type of chemical love— sometimes called "Limerence Love." There are other terms for it, but essentially, it's something that happens biochemically within our bodies.

Briefly: there's Phenethylamine (PEA), which acts like an amphetamine (the drug), along with the release of the chemical dopamine going around in your body. These chemicals can greatly influence your feelings. And then there is testosterone and other hormones mixed in with serotonin and the release of oxytocin that brings about most of this. It's even more technical than that, but I'll spare you the details. Just suffice it to say that the fluttery and surging highs that you experience in New Love are pushed to the forefront by a chemical reaction going on in your body.

Yes, you're attracted to certain things about this person. You obviously don't "fall in love" with everyone who comes your way. But the attraction is more complicated than it appears to be. It's kind of like the high you get from addictive substances. It can be a lot of fun, but the feeling isn't sustainable without the "help" of that substance. Certainly, the New Love high lasts longer than substance highs, but it's also not sustainable over the long run. It needs to be fed, or injected again. And it can also give you false readings. Things you wouldn't put up with normally seem to be less important until that high wears off and you wake up.

I remember this well when I "fell in love" with Steve. It's as though he could do no wrong. I overlooked and minimized things that I would never have with anyone else. One of the first things he did when we started dating is to cancel a date with me because he was "too tired." What? I would never have put up with that with anyone else. We were attending a college where there averaged nine guys to every gal. I didn't lack in having guys who wanted to take me out on any given night. I'm not bragging here, because neither did any other living, breathing gal at that college.

But I was attracted to Steve. And when he called me, I was miffed, but I overlooked it. And it's a good thing because we probably wouldn't be married to each other at this point if I hadn't. That is just one tiny example of the things I overlooked because of this very real biochemical reaction that was flowing through my body. And Steve overlooked a lot of my flaws and things that irritated him about me when we first were falling in "love." (I put the word "love" in quotation marks because we were actually falling more in "like" with each other, rather than falling in love. We didn't even know what love truly was until much later in our relationship.)

I believe Mark Twain had it right when he said:

> "Love seems the swiftest, but it's the slowest of all growths. No man or woman really knows what perfect love is until they've been married a quarter of a century."

That's where married love comes in. The commitment of marriage keeps you in the game (so to speak) as you work through your differences. When it is approached the right way, married love helps you to grow together as a couple, and grow up as individuals. At least, that's the way it's supposed to work. I like what Sam Levenson said:

> "Love at first sight is easy to understand; it's when two people have been looking at each other for a lifetime that it becomes a miracle."

And maintaining and growing love within marriage truly is a miracle. Blogger Ngina Otiende said, "That's why we make marriage vows and not wishes." Wishes can be forgotten, but our marriage vows are supposed to be continually before us in priority. Before God and a gathering of witnesses, we vow to love and cherish each other until death parts us. There is no secret clause in those vows that say that we love until…

Our Bridegroom, Jesus Christ, doesn't flit from one bride to the other. He is faithful to her (to us) through the trials of life, and He wants us to do the same with our bride or groom.

Grow Your Love

So, it's important to grow your love because New Love is not sustainable. The flutters eventually will go away. Yes, you can be madly in love with your spouse, even though you have been married a very long time. Steve and I have been married for more than forty-six years, and he can still get my heart beating wildly, just as it did when our love was new. But overall, our feelings towards each other have grown from the chemical high we experienced earlier in our relationship to a deeper, more lovely, and sustainable love. I really agree with the point Dr. Phil McGraw made on this matter. He said:

> "Falling in love is only the first stage of love. It's impossible to remain in that stage. A mature relationship will shift from dizzying infatuation to a deeper, more secure love. Don't make the common mistake of thinking that when the initial wild passion fades you aren't in love anymore. The answer is not to start a new relationship so you can recapture that emotional high with someone else. The answer is to learn how to move on to the next stages of love for a different but richer experience."
>
> - www.drphil.com
> Article, "Ten Relationship Myths"

And that's what I'm talking about here. You need to "move on" to grow your love and guard that, which you have and can have in the future—a richer love. On your wedding day, you publicly pledged your love to your spouse to continue to love. So do what you promised. Grow it.

But you also have to make sure you protect it. There are a lot of forces that can take it down. Most of them are hidden. That's why it's difficult to be aware that they are even there lurking to hurt your marriage. But they are. Just look around at other marriages that have failed. If they had grown and guarded their hearts, minds, and marriages, their love would be all the stronger and more vibrant.

So put emotional and mental hedges or fences around your heart to protect the sanctity you already have (and/or can have) in your marriage. God considers your marriage to be sacred. No outsiders are allowed into the inner circle of your partnership. Make sure you keep it that way.

Invest yourself in your marriage. Guard your heart from the invasion of others. I could give you all kinds of practical details about how to do this, but we have a lot of articles posted on the Marriage Missions website on this matter. It would be redundant to repeat those details. Take advantage of what we offer. Just put the word "guard" in our website search engine, and you can see what we have there to read. You will learn all kinds of practical ways to guard your heart, mind, and marriage.

Invasion of Tyranny of the Urgent, and the Media

I want to go down another road related to this matter at this time. It concerns the invasion of the tyranny of the urgent. It's something that pushes the spouse behind that which screams for attention the loudest. Please be aware of the problems of giving in to this type of invasion. Whenever possible, don't give in. Sometimes you need to, but don't let that be a way of life. It needs to be squelched when it threatens the sanctity of your marriage relationship. Marital needs won't always wait.

Waiting down this road is the invasion of other people through social media such as Facebook, texts, phones, emails, and the like. You don't have to physically be with someone to have them shove into your spouse's rightful place. Too many spouses are allowing themselves to be lured into investing their time with everyone and everything else other than their marriage partner.

It could be that you enjoy the high you get from the attention of others. I get that. But it can also be a trap that can push you too far away from your spouse. Or it could be that you feel lonely in your marriage. I'm not sure of the reason for that, but no matter what, you can't allow yourself to invest in that which can lure your heart to a place it shouldn't go. Please be forewarned that media, hobbies, taking care of too much stuff, paying closer attention to others than you should, even our friends, relatives, and children, can open your heart up to potential problems. Guard it with all diligence as God instructs to do in His Word (Proverbs 4:23).

You gave your heart to God. And on your wedding day, you also pledged your heart to your spouse. Those are covenant relationships—ones that should not be broken. Don't give it away to anyone else who tries to shove your spouse into the background. Your spouse should be your top priority right behind Jesus. And even then, Jesus wouldn't have you continually give your spouse only the leftovers of your time. Some leftovers are great. But a steady diet of it makes one wonder why they get second-place over and over again when others get your best.

Guard Your Mind

And that leads to the second part of this essential (although all three parts do overlap). Guard your mind from going places that it shouldn't. Curiosity and temptation can certainly grab at us and lure us to go places in our minds (and our bodies), even though we know that we shouldn't go there.

I used to love to watch Daytime Dramas on television (also called Soap Operas). I thought it was innocent fun to watch the drama of the presented plot. I thought, What does it hurt? Well, at first, it didn't hurt anything or anyone. But eventually, the Lord helped me to see that I was sometimes compromising my values in whom I was rooting for, and what I would allow myself to watch. Bed hopping was going on with "partners" who had no business being in bed with each other. Plus, I had no business watching anyone being in bed with each other in a sexual way.

Watching movies, and other media choices, plus reading magazines, etc., started to cause problems within my mind as well. Again, I found myself compromising my values. Plus, I found myself less satisfied with Steve. He didn't always act or say things the way these great lovers did. They set the bar high, and I failed to see that it set Steve up for failure in my eyes. He lacked having professional writers and coaches help him to say and do things as I thought he should. So I found Steve lacking (which in reality he really wasn't).

But then I woke up and saw the problematic mindset I was holding on to that was tainting the way I viewed our relationship. I came to the place where I knew I had to do a thorough cleaning and purging of that which I would allow to entertain me. I became more careful of what I watched and what movies I paid the theatres to see. Steve and I believe that when we purchase tickets to the theatre, we are putting in a vote as to the type of entertainment we want moviemakers to create. The same goes with books and magazines we purchase. I/we only want to put our vote in for clean entertainment—not that which will compromise our values. Guarding my mind becomes a lot easier when I'm not putting words and images into it that feed my sinful nature.

And the same goes for you. Do a sound and sight check on that which you feed your mind. Are there things you are letting into your eye gate and mind that you shouldn't? Throw the bums out.

Vow and work to do what we're told in Psalm 101:3-4 ESV:

> "I will not set before my eyes anything that is worthless. I hate the work of those who fall away; it shall not cling to me. A perverse heart shall be far from me. I will know nothing of evil."

Throw out the bad and flee as Joseph (of the Bible) did when someone who had evil intentions tried to tempt him with immorality. Then look for good things to put into your mind—especially as it concerns your spouse. It's the action of reject, dispose, and replace. It's also the action of "seek and you will find" as it pertains to looking for the good to focus on to replace the garbage that is offered.

I'll never forget a photo I saw in a newspaper a number of years ago. It was a picture of a big pile of garbage in the city garbage dump. Ewww!... You might think. But actually, it was quite profound because right in the middle of all of that land waste was a single white flower growing and thriving. It was truly a beautiful sight to see. As I looked at that picture, God spoke to my heart to let me know that even amidst the garbage, He still can provide beauty. But sometimes we have to look long and hard to see it. And sometimes we have to work long and hard to be it. We can be that little beauty growing amidst the mess if we put pure intentionality behind our motives, thoughts, and actions. It takes thoughtful effort to guard our hearts, minds, and marriages.

Slander and Pride

God's Word in Psalm 101:5, ESV brings out another point about guarding your mind. We're told:

> "Whoever slanders his neighbor secretly I will destroy. Whoever has a haughty look and an arrogant heart I will not endure."

What I see in that scripture, as it pertains to marriage, is to reject listening to or speaking about anything that would bash your spouse. Don't be prideful in thinking that you have it together more than he or she does, so it's okay to say things or listen to things about your spouse that you shouldn't. There is a lot of spouse bashing that goes on in today's world—especially on the wife's part. I know. I used to take part in doing that too.

But one day I was involved with my gal friends, and God seemed to turn up the volume within my mind so I could better hear what they were actually saying. It really boiled down to slander that they were speaking against their husbands. There was nothing that was wholesome about it at all. I'm pretty sure you know the scripture that brings this to light.

> "Do not let any unwholesome talk come out of your mouths, but only what is helpful for building others up according to their needs, that it may benefit those who listen."
>
> - Ephesians 4:29
> NIV

There was absolutely nothing wholesome or helpful being said about these husbands who were in the other room. I can't even start to think of any way it would build them up if they heard what was being said about them. And it certainly wouldn't benefit anyone who would listen. It would tickle their ears, and maybe their funny bones, but it wasn't innocent fun. It was pure slander.

I felt completely convicted and withdrew from the conversation. Eventually, when I was in other similar settings, I found ways of steering the talking points into other directions. I don't want to shame or blame, but rather substitute what's wrong for what's wholesome. I was wrong in doing it before, and I sure don't want to enable others to do the same. When I can I make a little joke of it, saying that we probably shouldn't go there, even if it seems to be fun. Most of the time the other gals giggle and agree, and we start to talk about other things.

I can't let my speech or my mind go to places where my husband is pushed into a bad place and I am pushed into a place where I appear to be better than him. I am not. And even if I was, that is for God to judge, not me. I am his partner—one who is called by God to spur him onto "love and good deeds" (as we're told to do in Hebrews 10:24).

I love what Ruth Graham said about her husband (evangelist) Billy Graham. She said, "It's my job to love Billy; it's God's job to make him good." It's not that we can't speak to spousal situations that are disturbing. We can, and should. "Speaking the truth in love" is a good thing for us to do for each (which is supported in Ephesians 4:15). But that's the point—we do that for each other. We are to be speaking the truth in love—motivated by love, not by pride, sinful anger, or any other unloving reason.

We can talk to a safe person (of the same sex) sometimes to get loving guidance when we are disturbed about something pertaining to our spouse. But our motives and the direction the conversation is steered in had better be motivated by love. It's good to think of Jesus standing in the room with us. If we would invite Him to sit at our table with us to be included in the conversation, then Love will guide us and help us. After all, the Holy Spirit is referred to in the Bible as "Our Wonderful Counselor" (Isaiah 9:6). He can guide the conversation in the healthiest of ways.

Beware of What You Feed Upon

Another area of the mind to guard is that which can cause you to starve out the good and give strength to the bad. Other people (such as family and friends) can say things about our spouse that we shouldn't feed upon, or even allow to be said in our presence. If they are saying things that are none of their business, or if they are saying things that prompt you to feel worse about your spouse than it is healthy to feel, then it's wrong.

Our spouse is supposed to be our first human priority. Other family members—our children, mom, dad, siblings, and others—fall in behind him or her. This is the "leave and cleave" principle presented in the Bible (Genesis 2:24; Matthew 19:5). Also, if anyone is causing division and you now feel more separated from your spouse than you should be, remember Jesus' words to not let anyone else "separate" us as husband and wife (Mark 10:9; Matthew 19:6).

If they're telling you that your spouse is cheating on you and they have proof—that's one thing. That is helpful information you need to know. But if they are saying slanderous things about your spouse, or they are calling him or her negative, mean-spirited names—then the conversation is sliding into the "it's none of your business" or the "I will not listen to this" category.

Talk to a wise, godly friend who is marriage-friendly, or a pastor or a counselor about those types if issues, not family members or "friends" who could try to steer you into an unwise direction. Be firm but polite, saying, "I just can't go there with you. That is between my spouse and me." Express love, but a "no thank you" attitude.

Read and embrace the principles given in your Bible. See what God tells you to do. Pray for your spouse, asking God for wisdom, as you need it. Take advantage of reading good Christian books; plus avail yourself of other info that can feed your mind in positive, wise ways of approaching pressing matters, rather than listening to gossip, slander, or opinions that are slanted against what God would have you do.

Guard Your Marriage

I told you earlier that this marriage essential slides all over the place as far as connecting the guarding of your heart, mind, and marriage. They truly intertwine. By guarding your heart and mind you are guarding your marriage. But I have a few more points I want to make on this issue concerning guarding your marriage.

One of them is to realize that we live in a world that is very unfriendly towards marriages. There are many more negative influences than ever before that can press in against us with the potential to seriously damage our marriages. These include entertainment choices, marriage-unfriendly friendships, people, places, and things we can spend our money upon, and get into debt over... just to name a few. We need to be wise in the daily choices we make.

On the other hand, however, we have many more positive influences available to us than ever before that are good and wholesome. These include going to church events and getting involved in Christian projects and such. These can be great to take advantage of when it works for us, as opposed to against us. I say that because even too much of a good thing is still too much. Make your choices wisely. Just because you can do something, it doesn't mean you should. Sometimes, it's best to leave it alone or let someone else do it so you can spend time growing in your love relationship with your spouse. Live your life together in a balanced way so everyone is happier.

Keep in mind that when you say yes to do things outside of the home, you are saying no to other things you can do with your spouse and your children. Sometimes, these other things are good; but other times they are not. Again, balance is key.

There are choices we must make to guard our marriages, and there are some people we need to guard ourselves against who can cause damage. We also need to be careful not to allow ourselves to slide into too much busyness (if we can at all prevent it). Many times when we are too busy, we let our guard down. We can snap at our spouse and others and respond in totally unkind ways. The saying I try to continually remind myself is that if I am too busy to be kind; I'm too busy. When I find myself being unkind because I'm in too much of a hurry all the time, I ask God to show me what I can eliminate from my schedule. God is faithful to help me do that when I ask. I need to guard my mind, mouth, and marriage; and you do too.

We need to set up some type of marital security system to keep the good in, and zap anything bad that tries to invade the sanctity of our marriages. Or maybe an alarm will go off when an intrusion is starting to take place. That would be ideal, wouldn't it? But God doesn't do that. He just tells us to "be on the alert" and draw close to Him so we are more aware of sinful intrusions. What it comes down to is that we must do things God's way, not ours.

"Friends"

Yes, even "friends" can be anything but true friends, when it comes to our marriages. Some friends were great when you were single, but now that you are married, they are a threat to your marriage. There is tension that is building between you and your spouse because of certain friendships. Friendships should be an asset to your life and marriage, not a deficit. They are to be encouragers, not discouragers.

Jay Kessler brings out this point in his book Family Forum:

> "Dr. Ted Engstrom, one of my spiritual mentors, told me once that every man needs both a Timothy and a Barnabas. That is, he needs a friend whom he can affect in a positive way—like Timothy. And he also needs someone like Barnabas, whom he can walk with, talk with, and share his innermost thoughts and feelings with."

There are friends who can be a "Timothy" and others who can be a Barnabas, who encourage us within our marriages. This goes for both husbands and wives. We need those types of friendships that can influence us in positive ways. We don't need the negative types of friendships. If they cause problems in our marriages, they really aren't our friends any longer. Perhaps they were good friends to have around when we were single, but they are not now.

A long time ago, the Lord made my husband and me aware of the importance of guarding our hearts and our marriage. This included being careful of the friends we allowed ourselves to get close to—whether it concerned friends of the same sex or the opposite sex. If this friend was any type of threat to our marriage, we realized it would be better to push the friendship away from us than continue on with it because of the importance of protecting our marital union. We decided to set marital boundaries with our friendships. We're glad we did, and we're glad we still do. Looking back, we have no regrets. And we certainly don't want to set ourselves up for regrets in the future.

We've seen it over and over again where "friends" or the spouses of friends get too "friendly." Eventually, we hear it told where they say to their spouses, "We never meant for it to happen." That's why it's better to set up boundaries ahead of time than to live in a world of regret later.

True Friends

The Scriptures are clear about the kind of friends we should have in our lives:

> "Better is open rebuke than hidden love. Wounds from a friend can be trusted, but an enemy multiplies kisses."
>
> - Proverbs 27:5-6
> NIV

That means that a friend will be honest with you, even if it hurts. That type of wound is temporary and is ultimately helpful. A friend won't pretend things are right when they aren't. They won't lead you to act or think in ways that you shouldn't. They won't antagonize your spouse, but will be a friend to you and to your marriage. And they won't step into your marriage in ways that will cause you to invest more in them, than investing in your marital partnership.

The marriage relationship is likened to a "cord of three strands" (Ecclesiastes 4:12). It's a relationship that God takes very seriously. And for that reason, so should you. Marriage is a living picture of Christ's love for the church (see: Ephesians 5:22-32) to a world that needs to see God's faithfulness lived out before them. That is serious business.

You may have had some great friendships going on like King David and Jonathan (as shown in the Bible). But sometimes the friends you had previously just aren't good ones for you to continue with at this stage of your life. As I said before, some friends are great ones when you are single, but they actually cause problems after you marry. Your priorities have changed, but theirs haven't.

We are to choose our friendships wisely. We're told in 1 Corinthians 15:33-34, NIV:

> "Do not be misled: 'Bad company corrupts good character.' Come back to your senses as you ought, and stop sinning; for there are some who are ignorant of God—I say this to your shame."

A healthy friendship will take on new dimensions once you marry. They will be supportive and will cheer you on in your married life to help your marriage, not hurt your marital relationship. If your friendship does not go in this direction, then you may need to let it go. That may be difficult to do. But if they are not able to walk with you in being supportive of your marriage through this season of your life, then that "close friendship" season is ended, and you need to withdraw from allowing them to be as close to you as they previously were.

Friendships That Corrupt

What once was good for a season doesn't always stay good for a lifetime. When fruit is ripe, it's good to partake of it. But when it turns rotten, then it's time to get rid of it. This same principle can apply to friendships.

Choose wisely the friendships you keep. And that is the emphasis I'm making here—friendships you "keep." When you marry, you are to give up your "single-minded" lifestyle. Keep in mind: "Above all else, guard your heart, for it is the wellspring of life" (Proverbs 4:23). Also, guard your mind against going places where it should not go. And prayerfully focus your thoughts on God would have you think about. "And the peace of God, which surpasses all understanding, will guard your hearts and your minds in Christ Jesus" (Philippians 4:7, NIV). By doing so, you protect your mind from the assaults that the enemy of our faith is trying to wage upon your heart, your mind, and your marriage.

Please realize that the enemy of our faith does not want your marriage to reveal and reflect the love of Christ. The mission of the enemy is to rip to shreds the "cord of three strands" that involves you, your spouse, and our God. Please guard your heart, your mind, and your marriage with all diligence.

Steve

> "With the divorce rate steadily climbing and infidelity creeping into even the happiest marriages, in a society that trivializes adultery and its devastating effects, with temptation and opportunity coming at you from all directions—how can you keep your marriage from becoming a statistic?"
>
> - Jerry B. Jenkins,
> "Hedges: Loving Your Marriage Enough to Protect It"

Within this marriage essential, Cindy and I want to cover an area that we see as one of the most critical areas in marriage—protecting it (to keep it from becoming a "statistic"). In the first three chapters, we covered Building a Solid Foundation; Being Intentional in Growing Your Love Relationship; and Invigorating Your Romance and Sex Life. If you take the steps outlined in those chapters you are well on your way to protecting your marriage from any onslaught the enemy of our faith can throw at you.

I can't tell you when it was that it hit me like a ton of bricks that I was doing little to nothing to protect my marriage. But I am so glad that God hit me upside the head and got my attention... letting me know that I needed to start reinforcing the hedges in my life to protect Cindy and myself from the attacks of the enemy of our faith.

To guard our heart, mind, and marriage means we have to watch out (be on the alert) for what I call the "big three" that can trip us up at any time. They are lust, anger, and pride. True, the enemy of our faith has many more "dirty tricks" to use to try to bring us down. But if we become successful at conquering these three areas, we will be light years ahead in protecting our marriages.

Lust Nearly Ruined Our Marriage

I loved my father. He was a great dad as I was growing up. He was my hero in many ways. He was a WWII veteran who had served in France after

D-Day. He taught me how to hunt and fish (neither of which I was good at). He was a hard worker and a great provider. However, he did like to look at pictures of naked women. It was my dad's "girlie magazines" that I discovered at the age of twelve that opened the door to an almost thirty-year addiction. From my very first exposure a switch went off in my brain similar to a cocaine addiction. I was hooked right from the beginning!

I was shy and awkward through my early teen years, which only caused me to withdraw even more into my fantasy world of airbrushed older women who "wanted" to have sex with me. They were always there and they always wanted to please me. I didn't have to be good looking to get a date. I didn't need to know how to talk to a girl. All I had to do was open the cover of the magazine, and I was able to get what I wanted. (Notice all the personal pronouns in this description. This is what sexual addiction will do to us. It does become all about ME, and what I want that can cripple us in our relationship with our wives.)

I did come out of my shell and developed a personality by the time I was seventeen or eighteen and began to date some. By the time I went to college I was still shy, but I had enough confidence to ask girls out. However, I never developed any long-term relationships until my sophomore year of college.

That's when I was a disc jockey on the campus radio station. On Friday, October 18, 1969, I was doing a request program trying to get people to call in and have me play a song. All my begging resulted in zero calls until I promised to reimburse the person the ten cents (for the payphone) to call in. (That shows how long ago this happened. It's been a long time since a phone call cost ten cents.)

To my delight, a really nice young woman (who later told me she felt sorry for me) called and made a request. We talked for about thirty minutes. She hung up; I played her song; and then she called back (this time it wasn't a "sympathy" call).

We talked for more than an hour, and before she hung up I asked if she had plans for the football game on Saturday. She didn't, so we set up a blind date. I asked her to meet me at the radio station and we'd go to the game from there. Because we didn't know what the other looked like, I had a couple of the guys "screen" her for me. I would be in the back room and they'd check her out. If she was attractive they were to come and get me. If they didn't feel she was attractive, they were to tell her I wasn't there. [NOTE: Yes, I know how shallow and immature I was! I'm not happy with what I did, but I'm glad for the outcome.]

My friend came back and told me, "Oh, you definitely want to come out to meet this girl!" And when I walked out and met Cindy for the first time, I felt my heart drop into my shoes. I'm surprised I could put sentences together when I started talking with her. She was a tall, drop-dead gorgeous redhead (and she still is all these years later).

She was way out of my league, but for some reason, we clicked (of course, now we know it was all God) and started dating. We had the usual lovers' spats and had time apart; but eventually, we got engaged and then married on March 18, 1972. Even so, all through this period of my life my porn addiction waxed and waned. I was even convinced that once Cindy and I were married and consummated our relationship, I would no longer be attracted to pornography. Wrong!

For more than twenty years in our marriage I struggled to stay pure. As you read our testimony earlier, I asked Jesus Christ to be my Savior and come into my life in 1974. I became even more convinced that now I would no longer struggle with this addiction. Wrong again!

I went into full-time ministry in 1978 with a Christian radio network and retired from there in May of 2016 after nearly thirty-eight years. In the years before my healing, I was overwhelmed with never-ending shame and guilt. I was afraid I'd be "found out" and fired.

Like most Christian guys who struggle with this, I would beg God and cry out to Him to take this from me. It was as though my prayers were bouncing off the ceiling. I was convinced that I was the only Christian guy in ministry, in my church, who had this problem. But then I went to the Promise Keepers conference in Boulder, Colorado, in 1994. Because I was broadcasting this event from Boulder back to our radio station in Detroit, I was sitting in the press box.

But I'll never forget when Promise Keepers founder, Bill McCartney, challenged the men who were battling with sexual addiction to come out of the stands and come forward to repent and pray. I started to weep as thousands of men went forward that night because I realized I was not alone. Because I was working I couldn't go forward, but I prayed the same prayer in the press box, and that was the beginning of my healing. The shame began to melt away. I felt empowered to be able to confess my sin and bring it out of the darkness and into the light. The enemy of our faith hates it when that happens in our lives, because the battle for our hearts is losing its grip.

I finally came to the realization that God wanted to heal me; but He needed me to participate—to put the work into it. And what He used for me to turn away from the porn for good was the book titled, "Every Man's Battle: Winning the War on Sexual Temptation One Victory at a Time" written by Stephen Arterburn and Fred Stoeker. I can't tell you why this made all the difference for me, but it just resonated with me, and the simple principles of statements such as "bouncing the eyes" was the key to my deliverance.

Something else I realized I had to do if I was going to remain pure and continue to live victoriously was to find a mature spiritual mentor to hold me accountable. There was one man, in particular, the Lord continued to impress on me to call; but I was afraid to call Al (Al Kuhnle was a man I'd known and respected for several years) and ask him to consider taking on this role.

He was a very important man in ministry where I lived at the time, and I thought, Why would a man like him "waste" his time on a man like me? It was the enemy of our faith trying again to shame me into thinking I wasn't worth it. These were all lies, which I bought for a while.

Al took me under his wing, and for more than five years he and I would meet monthly either face-to-face or by phone. I gave him permission to ask me five questions to hold me accountable in the areas I needed it the most:

1. Have you been spending regular time alone with the Lord in prayer and Bible study?

2. Have you spent time with Cindy, connecting with her in meaningful ways to meet her needs?

3. Have you been working out regularly to improve your physical fitness and taking care of your diabetes?

4. Have you been keeping your heart and mind pure from improper images, thoughts, or actions; and if not, what struggles have you had?

5. Have you lied to me about any of your previous answers?

The more I talked with Al about my addiction struggles, the easier it got to resist the temptations the enemy threw at me. I was emboldened to share my struggles openly with other men—even men I didn't know.

There's no doubt that I deeply regret all the pain my addiction caused in our marriage. But because I've confessed it all to Cindy and our sons, and have asked for forgiveness, I no longer feel the shame. Both Cindy and I have come to realize the importance of "Discerning the Difference Between the Conviction of the Holy Spirit and the Condemnation of the Enemy." In fact, we have an article, by that title, posted on our website that you can download for free and use as a tool for healing in your own life.

What I came to realize and would tell any man who is willing to listen is that if we never want to fall into sexual sin... or if we need to be delivered from sexual sin... it all starts with us. Besides God—me, myself, and I are the only ones who know what is lurking in our hearts and where we are most vulnerable to attack from the enemy of our souls. And knowing this means we must build hedges to guard our hearts and protect us.

Michael Hyatt wrote a leadership article that is posted on his website (www.Michaelhyatt.com) concerning the issue of why it is so important for leaders to guard their hearts (and it applies to all men). He gave three reasons why it is necessary to guard your heart. The first reason is:

> "Because your heart is extremely valuable. We don't guard worthless things. I take my garbage to the street every Wednesday night. It is picked up on Thursday morning. It sits on the sidewalk all night, completely unguarded. Why? Because it is worthless.
>
> "Not so with your heart. It is the essence of who you are. It is your authentic self—the core of your being. It is where all your dreams, your desires, and your passions live. It is that part of you that connects with God and other people.
>
> "Just like your physical body, if your heart—your spiritual heart—dies, your leadership dies. This is why Solomon says, 'Above all else.' He doesn't say, 'If you get around to it' or 'It would be nice if.' No, he says, make it your top priority."

I will add to what Hyatt said and go so far as to say that if your spiritual heart dies, your marriage can die too. So, what are we as men supposed to do? To expand a bit on what Michael Hyatt said, King Solomon gave us the answer several thousand years ago:

"Above all else, guard your heart, for everything you do flows from it."

- Proverbs 4:23
NIV

Solomon states in chapter 4, verse 1 of Proverbs: "Hear O sons, a father's instruction, and be attentive, that you may gain insight." So, this is a dad sharing his wisdom and heart with his sons (and to men for all future generations).

You may not have had a dad talk this honestly with you about the importance of guarding your heart as a man. If not, let me act in that role for a while here because I learned the hard way why this is extremely important. I think the following word picture can best illustrate what I need for you to understand.

Let me challenge all dads who have sons reading this: please don't abdicate your responsibility as a father to have a heart-to-heart with your son(s). I would say to start talking about this issue in an "age appropriate" manner by the time they are nine or ten. That's because research has shown the average age for first-time exposure to porn is around thirteen. Others say it's eleven. However, some boys were exposed as young as five.

Why is this so important? It's because children don't have the same mental capacity to evaluate the things that can harm them as adults can. Their brains haven't developed to that point. I can illustrate this through an experience I had with my oldest son, David.

When he was three we had an evening ritual. After dinner, he and I would walk to what he called the "sucker store" (convenience store). I would buy him a sucker and we would walk home. We would talk a little, but mostly he liked to explore everything along the sidewalk. What could have easily taken fifteen minutes to walk back and forth to the store often stretched into thirty to forty-six minutes.

One evening on our way home, he was sucking away on his sucker when he looked down and happened to notice a dandelion puffball. Apparently, he had never noticed these before, so he decided he wanted to examine it closely. He picked it and held it up close to his face. Next, he pulled the sucker out of his mouth. He began to examine both of them.

I could see the wheels spinning in his little head as he looked at the puffball and then the sucker. It's as if I could hear the words, "I know what this sucker tastes like. But I've never tasted one of these other 'suckers.'" I was so glad Cindy wasn't with us because she would have made some sort of "blech!" sound and told David to drop it. I, on the other hand, wanted to see how this played out. It's fun being a dad sometimes.

Sure enough, curiosity got the best of David, and he popped that puffball into his mouth. His expression was priceless and said it all: "I made a baaad mistake!" Amazingly, he survived his childhood in spite of me. When I got home and told Cindy about what happened, her expression was priceless too… after I got reprimanded for not stopping the "carnage" (LOL).

The moral of this story is that we can't just assume our children will make good judgments when they are faced with temptation. It may look good, but that doesn't mean that it is good. Porn looks harmless to those who are immature. But we know it isn't. You can do everything within your power to protect your children, but there's still the possibility that they will be exposed by other means beyond your control.

Even if you don't have Internet or TV in your home, their friends may have unprotected cell phones or devices at their fingertips. And all that has to happen is for your child to be shown something on their friend's device, and that could start the spiral downward into a serious problem of addiction.

Porn Equals Heart Disease in Christ's Body

What I've come to learn from my experiences is that porn attacks the heart of the Christian body. Let me explain. In July of 2016, I had what is referred to as the "widow-maker" heart attack. I was told that only 6 percent of the people who suffer the type of heart attack that I had survive. By the time I got to the hospital, my left anterior descending artery was 100 percent blocked. When the cardiologist/heart surgeon came in after looking at the EKG, he said that there was nothing he could do to open it. That's because the actual heart attack had happened several days prior to me going to the hospital. (It's a long explanation as to why I didn't go to the hospital immediately.)

The doctor did do a heart catheterization just to determine the extent of the damage. He said that 35 percent of my heart function was gone. So, they admitted me to Intensive Care to monitor my heart and were amazed at how quickly I began to recover. Less than thirty-six hours after they admitted me they discharged me, but with follow-up home care.

Even with my nothing less than remarkable recovery/healing, the doctor said I still needed to take precautions to reduce the risk of another heart attack or stroke. They weren't extraordinary measures, just common sense:

1. **Eat healthy**
2. **Exercise regularly**
3. **Reduce stress**
4. **Get adequate sleep**
5. **Take my meds**
6. **Get regular checkups**

A paramedic friend told me a couple of weeks into my recovery that I was "one lucky man." I told him, "No, I am one blessed man." He then said, "Well, somebody 'up there' must still have something for you to do because I don't normally see people who have what you had recover this way." Now, a year after my heart attack, I have pondered that maybe God healed me so that I could minister to those He brings my way.

Here's the parallel I see: just as heart disease kills millions of people every year, the number of marriages that die every year from what I call "porn disease" is staggering. In 2011 Psychology Today published the following statistic:

> "Every year for the past decade there have been roughly 1 million divorces in the United States. If half of the people divorcing claim pornography as the culprit, that means there are 500,000 marriages annually that are failing due to pornography."

Just as there are ways to prevent heart disease, there are also ways to prevent porn disease from occurring or from reoccurring. And the ways are remarkably similar to preventing heart attacks. Think of these points as ways to strengthen the hedges you need to protect your spiritual heart.

1. **Eat Healthy** —By this I mean be careful what you put into your heart and mind through your eyes. Be intentional to stay away from those "foods" (Internet, chat rooms, Facebook, workplace relationships, "innocent flirting") that can cause your heart to stray; and stay pure.
2. **Exercise Your Faith Regularly** —The more time you spend in the

Word and praying, the far less likely you'll be drawn away from your wife and into sexual sin. Another important component to getting and staying pure are regular times of worship. Don't isolate yourself from other Christ-followers. There really is strength in numbers. If that's not a good-enough reason, then follow what Scripture says: "Let us not neglect our church meetings, as some people do, but encourage and warn each other, especially now that the day of his coming back again is drawing near" (Hebrews 10:25, TLB).

3. **Reduce Stress** —Surprisingly this stands alone, just as for heart attacks. Research has shown that men are especially prone to succumbing to the temptation to view porn and masturbate when they are under stress. I also believe that it is equally important to find some "fun" things to do with your wife. If you both enjoy hiking, take a hike; if you both like movies, go to a movie and then out for coffee or dessert to talk about it. You get the idea. The more fun things you do together, the stronger your marriage will be. (We have a lot more ideas for you posted in the "Romantic Ideas" topic of our website.)

4. **Get Adequate Sleep** —Again, this is something that researchers found as a significant cause for men to fall into temptation. Being overly tired can lead to letting our defenses down, and not being aware or alert to the temptations the Devil will put in front of us. As I look back on my porn addiction days, numbers 3 and 4 were prominent in my times or moral failure.

5. **Take Your Meds** —I equate this to realizing you may need to see a counselor who has experience in working with people with sexual addiction. There is no shame in doing this. In fact, I believe any man who values his marriage enough to seek professional help for his sexual addiction is a hero. And it might mean actually taking "meds." I know some men who were prescribed anti-anxiety medications, such as Zoloft, because it can reduce the sexual urges to act out. These should not be taken unless your counselor feels it's a last resort to try to control your libido.

6. **Get Regular Checkups** —Here is where you need to find and meet with a mentor, minimally once a month to hold you accountable. This shouldn't be a "buddy" from work or church, but an older, more spiritually mature man who won't be afraid to call you out if you fail and give in to temptation. (I do this for a friend of mine who put

a porn filter on all of his devices. I get a regular email report from this ministry that tells me if this friend has viewed something he shouldn't. You can do the same with an accountability partner.) If you can't think of a man in your church that you could approach, ask your pastor for a suggestion. Ask God too, to show you who He thinks would be the best fit for you. Because God is even more invested in your healing, He will provide and answer to this prayer.

Men, there are so many resources at our fingertips today that there is absolutely no excuse you can give for remaining in this destructive lifestyle. I have yet to talk to a man who was delivered from this trap completely on his own. There are many Christian-based programs that have had great success in helping men get unhooked. You can find a long list of recommended resources in the pornography and cybersex section on our website.

If you are even wondering if you have a problem with pornography, you owe to yourself, your wife and your family to at least go to our website and look at the section to see if there's anything there that resonates with you.

Now, if you're saying, "I know I don't have a problem with porn," then praise God. But there are other forms of lust that can be equally destructive to the marriage relationship.

I want to talk briefly about one of the biggest threats to marriage today— the "workplace romance." We have an article on our website that talks extensively about the dangers here. It's called "The Workplace Romance: The New Infidelity."

In this article, marriage counselor Shirley Glass says she discovered in her practice that fifty percent of the unfaithful women and about sixty-two percent of unfaithful men she treated were involved with someone from work.

> "Men and women who work closely together under stressful conditions can quickly become attracted to one another. They often share interests over coffee or lunch getting to know one another. One researcher calls this new kind of affair the 'cup of coffee' syndrome.
>
> "Men and women begin with safe marriages at home and friendships at work. As they regularly meet for these breaks, relationships develop into deep friendships. Coworkers come

to depend on these coffee trysts. Soon they have emotional work friendships and crumbling marriages.

"Longer work hours also contribute—especially when companies promote 'teamwork,' encouraging close working relationships between team members. This makes for a romantically conducive environment."

- www.shirleyglass.com

At the bottom of that particular article on the website, we received a comment from Eugene in South Africa. He summed up better than I could on how we men need to approach this subject:

"The best, and I think only possible way, to avoid any kind of affair (office or not) is the following of what I had learned through my mistake and the grace of God. I did not have an affair, but because of my friendship with the "other" woman, it was bound to happen. I realized if I can't tell my spouse about my friendship with this lady... then this friendship is wrong. If I don't feel comfortable talking to her when I am at home with my spouse, then I have nothing to say to her when I am alone.

"As a man I know we have a lot of 'reasons' (which I now call excuses) for why we started to have an affair. But I believe there is no good enough 'reason' (excuse) to have an affair. If she doesn't understand you... pray about it. If she doesn't understand your sexual needs, talk to her or a counselor. She always nags... have you sat down and listened what is she nagging about? Maybe, just maybe, it's because you are not doing what you promised to do. In closing... if your relationship is right with your Heavenly Groom... your relationship with your earthly bride will be blessed."

I'll be perfectly blunt here—if you are currently involved with another woman, end it now! If you are flirting with another woman, stop it now!

The destruction and fallout from this kind of illicit relationship will go on for years, and perhaps generations. Remember what the Bible says, "But if you fail to do this, you will be sinning against the Lord; and you may be sure that your sin will find you out" (Numbers 32:23, NIV).

I'm going to close this section on lust with a quote I heard that resonated with me. I hope it inspires you as well:

> "Freedom is never won in a single battle. It's something we have to fight for every day."
>
> American soldier who fought to liberate France from the Germans in 1944

The second part of the "big three" I referred to earlier is we need to guard our hearts from anger.

> "A moment of patience in a moment of anger prevents a thousand moments of regret."
>
> - Chinese Proverb

And the Bible says:

> ". . . Everyone should be quick to listen, slow to speak and slow to become angry, because human anger does not produce the righteousness that God desires"
>
> James 1:19-20
> NIV

> "Be not quick in your spirit to become angry, for anger lodges in the heart of fools."
>
> - Ecclesiastes 7:9
> ESV

I love it when the philosophers of the world write (like Chinese proverbs) and it supports God's word. The Bible has more than thirty verses that talk about anger. So, if the Bible addresses a topic that many times, then we really need to pay special attention. Obviously, I can't cover everything we need to know about this subject in this chapter. My goal is to just make you, as a couple, aware that unresolved anger in your marriage can destroy it.

> "Those who have studied anger indicate that more anger is developed in marriage relationships than in any other relationship where people are involved. Unresolved anger is the principal cause of violence toward another person. Successful anger management can mean the difference between marital joy or absolute misery. The success or failure of a marriage may

depend on the way a couple copes with their angry feelings."

StrongerMarriage.org
article, "Dealing with Anger in a Marriage"

Note that the key to success or failure of a marriage is directly tied to how you cope/resolve your angry feelings.

David and Vera Mace, who are pioneers in the Marriage Enrichment movement, write about how to cope with angry feelings:

> "When you feel angry, express your anger in words, stated calmly, and with love. Use much the same tone, as you would say 'I'm tired,' or 'I'm very tired.'
>
> "Couples who effectively manage their anger agree that it is necessary to express and acknowledge it. They agree never to attack in anger, even though they share angry feelings. They should agree with each other that they won't yell at one another unless there is extreme danger.
>
> "If a firm, no-yelling policy is developed, it will remove the need for a spouse to feel defensive or to develop any type of retaliatory anger. If both partners can express their anger calmly, they are better able to find out how and why the anger is present in the marriage."

Now, admittedly, if either of you in your marriage is frequently having angry outbursts, then, by all means, seek the help of a good "marriage-friendly" counselor. Cindy and I will address the subject of fighting in the explanation after the next marriage essential.

You can find articles such as "Explosive Anger in Marriage," When Anger Becomes Abuse," "War of Words In Marriage," as well as suggested resources to help in this area on our website.

However, remember that you can read all the good advice in the world, but if you don't apply what you learn, the info does you no good. We hear from hundreds of people every year who come to us looking for help because anger in their marriages has turned to either verbal or physical abuse (sometimes it's the husband and sometimes it's the wife). But many of them never follow through in applying what they have learned that can change their marriage. So, what good is it?

Remember God's admonition to us: "Refrain from anger and turn from wrath; do not fret—it leads only to evil" (Psalm 37:8, NIV).

The last of the big three that I want to caution you about as it relates to guarding your heart, mind, and marriage is pride.

> "In truth, pride is double-edged: destructive and ludicrous in the wrong place and the wrong proportions, but heroic and admirable in the right ones."
>
> - Dr. Steve Aicinea
> The Sport Journal

What Dr. Aicinea says is even backed up by Scripture. There's no doubt the Bible most often refers to pride as a "destructive force" in our lives... "Pride goes before destruction, a haughty spirit before a fall" (Proverbs 16:18, NIV). But the other "edge of the sword" says: "Each one should test their own actions. Then he can take pride in himself, without comparing himself to somebody else" (Galatians 6:4, NIV).

I'm not going to belabor this point, but I feel it's important to help you have clarity on what really matters... our total and utter dependence on God each and every day to live our lives in such a way that we bring glory and honor to Him. And this is especially true in our marriages.

If you think you don't need God's help, my friend, in staying pure in your thoughts and actions, in controlling your anger... and any one of a hundred other traps that can kill your marriage, then you have a pride issue.

> "In his pride the wicked man does not seek him; in all his thoughts there is no room for God."
>
> - Psalm 10:4
> NIV

If you just felt a piercing in your heart as you read that verse, that's the Holy Spirit telling you that you need to make a course correction. I can honestly say that if I had not surrendered my life to God by asking Jesus Christ to be my Lord and Savior in October of 1974, there is absolutely no way Cindy and I would be married today... which means there would be no Marriage Missions International.

One of my constant prayers reflects that I know I can't do anything without God's help. I confess my weakness and propensity to try to take control of my life. I pray that in all my ways I will acknowledge Him and He will keep my paths straight. (See: Proverbs 3:6.)

I hope you will apply these principles in your life and test God to see if He will be true to His Word in helping you "Guard Your Heart, Mind, and Marriage."

MARRIAGE ESSENTIAL #5
FIGHT THE GOOD FIGHT
RESOLVE CONFLICT IN HEALTHY WAYS

This marriage essential may sound like an oxymoron—because how in the world can we "fight a good fight?" Most of us will do just about anything to avoid a fight, disagreement, conflict, argument, controversy, etc., in our marital relationship. But they are inevitable. Whenever you put two very different people together in close proximity for an extended period of time, something will eventually arise that can lead to a fight. Our hope is that what we share will enable you to learn some principles to help resolve conflict without one of you walking away feeling you're in a state of "ruin."

Steve

"Ironically, concepts revealed in The Art of War, a book written in the sixth century B.C., helped us resolve our battle against selfishness—and seek peace. The advice offered by Chinese philosopher-general Sun Tzu to his trainees can also help you fight to improve your marriage. As recorded in the book, Tzu noted: '[War] is a matter of life and death, a road either to safety or to ruin. Hence it is a subject of inquiry which can on no account be neglected.' If you replace the word war with marriage, the message is profound for couples."

- Dr. Greg Smalley,
Focus on the Family
Article, "Marriage Is a Battle... but Not Against Each Other"

I totally agree with that statement. Over the course of our marriage, Cindy and I have fought about almost everything there is to fight about from A-Z (apple pie to zoo visits—I'm not kidding). I dare say we have gone around so many times it reminds me of the old cowboy adage: "If the horse is dead, dismount!"

It took many years of trial and error—successes and failures—before we finally figured it out. Here is a moment of transparency: We are much better at identifying conflict and dealing with it in healthy ways. But that doesn't mean we're perfect. Just the other night Cindy said something very innocently; I took it the wrong way and stomped out of the room. About fifteen minutes later (that's how long it took me to get out of my "jerky" mood) I went to Cindy and asked her forgiveness.

We made mad, passionate love for an hour and everything was good. Here's another moment of transparency: That is a slight exaggeration. We actually made up and watched TV together. But at our age, that's almost the same thing. They both bring pleasure (albeit different levels of pleasure).

In Greg Smalley's article, he remarked on the war example from General

Sun Tzu and said, "If you replace the word war with marriage, the message is profound for couples." Cindy and I both couldn't agree more. So, let me restate it this way:

> [Marriage] "is a matter of life and death, a road to either safety or ruin. Hence it is a subject of inquiry which can on no account be neglected."

Undoubtedly, most, if not all of you would say you want to pursue a road to safety in your marriage. Few people enter into their marriage thinking, "Let's pursue a road to ruin." It's one thing to want to pursue a road to safety, but how do we do this? For Cindy and me, our road to safety in our marriage was one filled with potholes (arguments) and big bumps (misunderstandings). Neither of us grew up in homes where we had good role models for resolving conflict. So, we entered our marriage with a deficit in good communication and problem-solving skills... and we never knew we were lacking. We just thought we would escape this because our love was different. Does this sound familiar?

In the nearly twenty-one years I lived at home, I never once heard my mom and dad argue. I saw them become irritated at each other occasionally, but I never experienced them arguing. So, conflict resolution was a foreign concept to me. As a result, when Cindy and I started dating and conflict entered our relationship, I had no coping skills, and definitely no skills in how to resolve our arguments in healthy ways. My way of "handling" these times is that I would shut down. I would literally retreat and go to sleep. I brought this style of problem-solving into our marriage. As you can imagine, this was a major pothole (argument) in and of itself. Here's why.

Cindy grew up in a home where she saw her parents fighting all the time. They had screaming matches, but she never saw them resolve the problem. She never saw one ask for forgiveness or even say, "I'm sorry." Then as a teenager, she saw her dad walk out on her mom for another woman, leaving her mom, her, and her three siblings virtually destitute.

By the time we met in college, her dad had returned to the home and to the marriage. While Cindy was happy for her mom, she had a hard time trusting and respecting her dad for many years. It also meant she had a hard time trusting other men—even me. So, when I would retreat and go to sleep rather than face the argument head-on, Cindy saw this as a threat to being abandoned, which brought about a lot of fear for her. It took many years for us to put all the pieces of this puzzle together to give us the understanding we have today.

If you remember our personal story from what we wrote under Marriage Essential #1, after I was diagnosed as a Type-1 diabetic, the level of conflict/arguing in our marriage escalated. And not having the tools or understanding of how to resolve these problems, they became insurmountable to Cindy, which led to our separation. As Cindy tells women, "Actions motivated by fear never go in a good direction." But it's all she knew at the time.

Fortunately for us, God had another plan, and after we surrendered our lives and marriage to Him, He began the process of growing our marriage the way it needed to be. The two biggest areas we needed help in were communication skills and conflict resolution. These two go hand-in-hand. The better you can communicate clearly your needs and wants, the less likely they will become points of conflict.

I think it's safe to say that most of us grew up with very little, if any, good examples in conflict resolution. We didn't see many examples of good communication skills being used between our parents. At least Cindy and I didn't. That's why we say all the time that even if you didn't have a good example as you were growing up, it's important that you become a good example to all who see your marriage lived out every day.

Before we get into some of the marriage-changing principles that helped Cindy and me, I want to challenge you to examine your heart first. This is because all of the resources in the world won't help you one iota if you aren't willing to change what's "not working." Here's where to start.

Don't Settle for Less Than God's Best

> "Few people attain great lives, in large part because it's just so easy to settle for a good life."
>
> - Jim Collins
> "Good to Great"

When I read the book "Good to Great" a number of years ago, I thought, Wow! These principles aren't only to move individuals and businesses forward, but they can also move marriages forward. Here's what God impressed on my heart when I read the book:

Few couples attain great marriages because it's so easy to settle for a good marriage. I sincerely believe this because that's exactly where I was in the past. I was content to say that my marriage was "good." This was mostly because I was lazy... and it was easier to settle for good.

Often, we men will think things are good in the marriage when our wives have a completely different perspective. But because there may be no fighting going on at the moment, we can interpret that as a "good marriage."

A definition of what I used to think made a marriage "good" comes from Pastor Scott Engleman's study called "The Genesis of Marriage." "Many say, 'Marriage is two people seeking a peaceful co-existence together with the hope of obtaining a measure of personal happiness.'" On the surface there doesn't seem to be anything wrong with that, right?

If we want to move our marriages from good to great (or even bad to great), we want to dispel the myth that conflict is bad for your marriage. What's bad is when a marital conflict escalates into:

1. **Raised voices** - Arguments should never elevate above a normal tone of voice. Think of it this way, if the front door to your house was open and your neighbors were walking by, they shouldn't be able to tell if you're arguing.

2. **Any form of abuse** - Verbal—i.e., screaming in one's face, using profanity; or physical abuse: this includes pushing, shoving, slapping, throwing things, punching walls, etc.

3. **Name calling**

4. **Threats** - Including using the "D" word... "Divorce."

Sadly, in the past, Cindy and I were guilty of many of these escalations. (Clarification: though we never hit each other, we did do a lot of yelling.) All of the above are sins against each other, but more importantly, they are sins against our God.

So, what made the difference for us? It wasn't one big event that brought about the change. It was a series of ways God started to reveal to us His precepts for the need to learn effective conflict resolution skills. Let's face it, if God dumped everything on us that we need to know all at once, it would be so overwhelming that our brains would explode.

One of the major turning points for us was when we both took a

Temperament Analysis offered by our church. At first, it seemed silly, and I didn't really believe it would help us in any way. But when we got the results, it was as if God turned on the lights as we really saw who we are.

Briefly, Temperament Analysis is one of the most basic tools that have been used for centuries to gain insight into our personalities and why we do what we do. There are four basic types: sanguine, phlegmatic, melancholy, and choleric. There are free tests online that you can take to gain the same insight that Cindy and I did. Here's what we discovered about ourselves, and each other (the description of our temperaments is found on the website: www.thetransformedsoul.com):

CINDY: Melancholy/Sanguine

"They are detailed, creative, and organized; the Melancholy is tempered by the outgoing and warm Sanguine. A Melancholy/Sanguine makes an excellent teacher, as their organized side is well versed in the facts and their Sanguine side makes them enjoyable to listen to. He/she is an emotional, sensitive person, who feels the pain of others. They can go from being moved to tears to being critical and hard on others. Both temperaments can be fearful, which may make this an insecure person with a poor self-image. But they are highly talented, which they don't often see within themselves."

STEVE: Phlegmatic/Sanguine

"This is the easiest to get along with being congenial, happy, and people-oriented. They make excellent administrators and other jobs that involve getting along with people. However, he/she may lack motivation and discipline and may fall short of their true capabilities. They would much rather go for the fun, rather than work. He/she may 'putter around' for years without making progress. They often prefer stability to uncertainty and change. They are consistent, relaxed, calm, rational, curious, and observant, qualities that make them good administrators. They can also be passive-aggressive."

For Cindy and me, this is what God used to give us both insights into why we would argue/fight about different things. For example, it used to drive me to distraction because Cindy was so detailed, organized, and a perfectionist. And I never understood why she had such a hard time accepting my compliments. But I better understand it now.

She, on the other hand, never understood why I rarely took things seriously. I would tease and joke around—a lot (actually too much at times). And it drove her nuts that I wasn't disciplined. She actually thought I "plotted" ways to evade issues and upset her. But I didn't. And she now better understands this, as well, because of the analysis.

Opposites Attract and Opposites Can Divide

When we sat down and started discussing what was brought into the light, we realized that the traits we possess are what attracted us to each other to begin with. But now that we had to live with these traits day in and day out, we also realized they could divide us—if we focused on the negative aspects of our personality traits.

We could have both looked at each other and said, "Well, that's just the way God made me. There's nothing I can do about that; so learn to live with it." That would have been the "road that led to ruin" in our marriage as talked about above. Instead, we chose the "road that led to safety." That wasn't an easy road to take, but we both realized it was the road the Lord chose for us. The first step on that road was to identify where we had hurt each other along the way and to ask for forgiveness. And then we invited God in to help us change what needed to be changed.

For me I knew I needed to start by working on my teasing and the things I would sometimes say to Cindy that hurt her. The more time I spent in the Bible, I began to see things I hadn't realized before. An example comes from Ecclesiastes 10:12-13, NIV: "Words from a wise man's mouth are gracious, but a fool is consumed by his own lips. At the beginning his words are folly. At the end they are wicked madness—and the fool multiplies words." And also, "Do you see a man who speaks in haste? There is more hope for a fool than for him" (Proverbs 29:20, NIV). "If anyone considers himself religious and yet does not keep a tight rein on his tongue, he deceives himself and his religion is worthless" (James 1:26, NIV).

This was the beginning of the end of so many arguments and hurt feelings.

What surprised us is that such a simple tool could accomplish so much. Of course, we know it was God using this tool in our lives.

Another aspect of all of this is we learned how to use our "differences" to work for us rather than against us. For example, because Cindy is such a detail person, she has helped me to organize areas where I have needed it the most. Her creativity helps me too—something I often lack. I came to see that she isn't being "picky," but rather this is actually one of her strengths that can benefit me. Plus, my parents loved her right from the beginning because she helped me to become a more serious student in college. She had a scholarship and studied a lot, so if I wanted to be with her, I had to study more. And even now, I read more, do more serious ministry work, and am more knowledgeable because she has helped to stretch me intellectually over the years.

On the other hand, Cindy came to see that my sense of humor could help her find balance when she leans towards being too serious. I am able to help her to relax and enjoy life more. She has a great sense of humor, but I help her to find it when it is buried by the serious stuff she gravitates towards. She takes on less of a workload (which she should), and I take on more responsibilities, which I know I should. We balance each other well.

Together, we lighten each other's loads and fill in the details of life. We have learned to combine our talents and differences to make them work for us, instead of fighting against them and because of them. God knew we could be good together. We just needed to get onto His plan for us, rather than our own.

We challenge you, as a couple, to find a way to examine your differences, rejoice that God made you different... and then take the time to learn how to make those differences work FOR you and not become points that work against your marriage.

Passive Aggressive Behavior

I also want to make sure to address the last little phrase that describes a phlegmatic... "They can also be passive-aggressive." I know that didn't escape the attention of a number of you. It certainly didn't escape Cindy's attention. When we first saw it, we didn't really know what it was, so we studied up on it. I have to admit there were many times I used a passive-aggressive approach in dealing with conflict. Briefly, for clarity in what I'm talking about, here's a good description:

> "The passive aggressive will say one thing, do another, and then deny ever saying the first thing. They don't communicate their needs and wishes in a clear manner, expecting their spouse to read their mind and meet their needs. After all, if their spouse truly loved them he/she would just naturally know what they needed or wanted. The passive aggressive withholds information about how he/she feels; their ego is fragile and can't take the slightest criticism. So why would they let you know what they are thinking or feeling?"
>
> - Cathy Meyer
> www.about.com
> Article "Passive Aggressive Behavior, a Form of Covert Abuse"

That pretty much described me a lot of the time. The areas that were the biggest problems for me were that I would withhold information about my feelings; my ego was extremely fragile and I hated criticism. And these were not easy patterns for me to break. First, I had to ask God to help me learn the trigger points that would bring these on and then deal with the conflict head-on, rather than mentally run away from them.

We have several articles on our website that address this subject. Let me just say that as you're reading this and you feel a "prick" in your spirit, it may be God saying this is you and it's time for you to address it... as He did with me.

Before you relegate this information to psychobabble or gobbledygook, ask God if He wants to use a tool like this in your marriage to unlock some of the "secrets" that have plagued the misunderstandings in your relationship for so many years. There are so many different tests/inventories available today that can provide the help and insight you may need to change things. We like the Basic Temperament Analysis because you can take it yourself and not necessarily need a counselor to help you interpret the results.

However, don't hesitate to involve a (marriage-friendly) counselor in areas where you struggle to resolve painful issues. Throughout our marriage, there were times when Cindy and I realized we were at loggerheads on an issue and couldn't agree on a solution. That's when we'd take it to a counselor who could look at both sides objectively and give us advice as to how to resolve it.

We have an article posted on our website titled "Choosing a Marriage Friendly Counselor." We encourage you to read it before you select a counselor to help you with your marriage.

"Good is the enemy of that, which is great." That's what Jim Collins said in his book Good to Great. What Cindy and I have come to know is that God never intended for us to just settle for anything less than His best. Think about this for a moment: the enemy of our faith wants us to believe that good is good enough. He wants us to believe that if there doesn't happen to be any conflict going on "right now," then that's good enough. It's the enemy that wants us to just "settle."

Why is all of this so important? The obvious reason is because "a great marriage" is what God wants for all of us. We also have said before that it's important for your children to see this modeled so that when they become adults and get married they will understand what a healthy marriage looks like.

There's one more very important reason we need to work to make our marriages "great" that God showed Cindy and me: if we "Reveal and Reflect the Heart of Christ Within Our Marriage," it will draw others to Him. That is the mission objective of Marriage Missions International, and we believe it should be for all of us within our marriages.

In 1988 I took a ministry transfer to another city. On the Sunday our pastor announced this to the congregation, a young couple came up to us after the service and said, "You don't know us, but we've sat further back behind you for several years. We're a quieter couple. But we've watched how the two of you interact with each other, and we just want you to know that we have often said to each other that we want a marriage just like yours." As Cindy and I were driving home, we started to process what this couple had just said. We couldn't think of anything "outstanding" we had done that would cause them to think that.

Then we realized we didn't have to have done anything outstanding. Our love and respect for each other had grown to the point that we were living it out consistently—all of the time. We didn't live one way in public and another way behind closed doors. No matter where we were we would always sit as close to each other as possible. I would have my arm around her (yes, even in church) or hold her hand—even when we were standing during praise and worship songs. I often look over at her and mouth the words, "I love you." And she would respond in kind. We aren't putting on a "show" to try to impress anyone; it's what flows naturally from our hearts. When this couple expressed this to us, we felt the pleasure of God. It was as though He gave us a hug and said, "I'm proud of you."

Eleven years later we were about to take another ministry transfer and the pastor of our church at the time made a similar announcement. Immediately following the service, two young women approached Cindy and me, and it was like déjà vu. They too had been sitting behind us for several years, observing us. The only difference was they said they were both single, but when they did marry, they "wanted a marriage just like ours." On the way home, we just smiled at each other and thanked God that He allowed us to be a witness for Him that He cares so much about marriage.

Cindy and I would love to fix every communication and conflict problem you have in your marriage. But because we haven't fixed every problem in ours yet, the best we can do is share with you what has helped us find tremendous healing and success. That's why we created the Marriage Missions website.

Please remember our goal should be to "Fight the Good Fight." For additional help and resources on this subject, go to our website at www.Marriagemissions.com and look in the "Communication and Conflict" and "Communication Tools" topics.

In Steve's portion of this essential, you read about the conflicted way we entered into our marriage. We didn't realize that we would drag the different ways we saw conflict handled while growing up in our own marriage. And we were the ones who did the dragging. Our love, which we thought would help us conquer all, didn't help us at all. We assaulted it with arguing in unhealthy and unloving ways. As a result, we eventually didn't even like each other, let alone love each other.

Right Fighting and Marathon Arguing

The love we thought we had for each other was becoming a distant memory. It was being trashed and shoved out by the childish ways we handled our conflicts. We got involved with "right fighting" with each other. Right fighting involves a "winner takes all" attitude, making you (think you're) the winner and your spouse is the loser. It also involves arguing to such a degree that you would much rather prove you are right than to salvage the relationship.

Sadly, we both were involved in doing this. We now know that this was so very wrong. It's like what Dr. Phil McGraw said on one of his television programs:

> "Everyone who thinks they're 'winning' an argument needs to consider how it's affecting their partner. Think about it—how can it be a winning situation if in order for you to win, your spouse has to lose?"

It makes no sense at all. We see that now. But we sure didn't back then. So now we really work hard not to do that. I wouldn't be a good marriage partner if I wanted to make my husband out to be a loser. And I certainly don't want to be seen as a loser either.

That is a good reason why right fighting should be thrown out of marriages. We need to act as though we are on the same side—because we are supposed to be. Spouses vow to marry each other on their wedding day. That includes marrying our differences so they do not cause us to be separated in our resolve to love and honor each other.

Sure, we can have differences. But we shouldn't allow these differences to get us to the place where we treat each other as though we are enemies or opponents driven to win no matter what the costly emotional, psychological, and spiritual expense to our spouse. Too often we can allow our differences, in the ways in which we fight, cause division at the expense of annihilating our spouse's feelings.

> "Marriage is sacred. Couples are going to have differences and fight. The point of marriage is to stand together and confront that together."
>
> - Sheila Wray Gregoire

Standing together and confronting whatever is separating us is important. We can confront in love, and even differ in our approaches and opinions. But within those differences we need to find ways to bridge our differences, rather than allow ourselves to build emotional walls of separation.

What's also sad is that Steve and I were also involved in a lot of marathon arguing. Our arguments would go on, and on, and on, and on. We really should have taken breaks if we couldn't work things out. Marathon arguing can be exhausting, and it can throw the tension going on between us over the top. Steve and I cared more about getting the other to concede to doing things our way, or agreeing with us, than resolving the conflict. I'm ashamed to even think about how nasty our arguments would get at times.

And forget about our differences being resolved in healthy ways. We didn't even think about that as a possibility. Of course, we figured our own angle of looking at and approaching things was the right way. As far as we were concerned, that was the healthy way. But it wasn't. It was foolish.

And Fools, We Were!

We're told in the Bible:

> "A fool gives full vent to his anger, but a wise man keeps himself under control."
>
> - Proverbs 29:11, NIV

> "A fool's mouth is his undoing, and his lips are a snare to his soul."
>
> - Proverbs 18:7 NIV

> "A fool finds no pleasure in understanding but delights in airing his own opinions" (Proverbs 18:2, NIV). "Even a fool is thought wise if he keeps silent, and discerning if he holds his tongue."
>
> - Proverbs 17:28 NIV

Looking at just those scriptures alone, yep! We were fools. Giving voice to our anger at each other was our goal, not resolving our conflicts. We thought it was our goal, but as we look back at the way we fought, it wasn't. There certainly was no healthy "marrying" going on in our lives together when we were upset.

I really had an "ah-ha moment" when I read something written by Tyler Ward. He was recounting something his marriage mentor told him when he and his wife were going through a rough time. He wrote:

> "What is needed to accomplish the marrying of lives is to practice a method of resolving (read: RE-SOLVING) the situation through communication."
>
> - Tyler Ward
> "Marriage Rebranded'

Did you get that? To resolve conflict within marriage, you have to marry your lives together and re-solve the problem at hand. It isn't about getting my way or my spouse's way, but our way—together. As someone once said, "In marriage, we won't always think alike, but we need to think together." I have the situation solved in my mind one way, and Steve has it solved in his mind another way. But the conflict at hand shows that somehow we need to solve it together in a way that works for both of us. It should be done in such a way that our fights don't end up in us insulting or assaulting each other.

Re-solving Our Differences

And to do that, we need to talk to each other—not at each other, and we need to listen—really hear what each of us is trying to communicate. If we don't do that, how can we re-solve the problem at hand? Steve and I had to learn how to stop talking at each other, slow down our talking (so we don't say what we shouldn't), and actually listen to what the other person was saying with and without words. And perhaps you need to as well. Think about it.

This hasn't been easy for us. After years of approaching conflict in unhealthy ways, we've had to learn and un-learn some bad habits to change the ways we approach our differences. And that has been a challenge, to say the least. Old habits die hard. It's not too difficult to fall back into old patterns. But our marriage relationship is so much better, healthier, and loving because we have and are doing what we need to, so we implement positive changes. Remember the essential about intentionality being a key piece in lasting change. That goes a long way in choosing to un-learn those bad habits.

A big part of this success is because we both feel heard and validated now in how we communicate our true feelings. We feel that our viewpoints matter to each other. We are a marital team—not two independent people living in the same house talking to and screaming at each other. But this wonderful change has come with time and effort.

Someone once said, "Change happens by inches, not miles." And that has been true for us. However, every inch forward has been well worth it. Our marriage is so good now. How I pray this for each person that reaches out to get the help needed. Positive change can happen. Even if the dysfunction has been going on for years and years. You can bring about positive change with the Lord's direction, and your application of what you need to do to bring about this change.

There are so many things I'd love to share with you concerning this marriage essential to "fight the good fight." Actually, there is more helpful marriage advice that is available to us than ever before. The problem is that we may read or listen to it, but we stop short of applying it. We don't connect the dots that after getting the info, we are to glean from it, and then apply what we can use. We can have all the tools in the world to fix what is broken available to us for our use, but if we don't actually use them, they're useless. It all just becomes empty words that go nowhere.

Even if your spouse won't do his or her part, don't let that stop you. You aren't accountable for your spouse—you are only accountable for what you do. In the Garden of Eden, God didn't listen to Adam's lame excuse, "It's the woman You gave me..." And God won't listen to our excuses either. He will deal with our spouse's actions on His terms later. And He will deal with us on His terms without our spouse being present. You are to focus your attention on what you do, and what you alone don't do. Blame-shifting is what children do.

But marriage is for grownups, not children. When you married, you entered into an adult world, whether you realized it or not. Spouses need to act like adults and deal with their own issues, and hopefully, help each other deal with theirs in positive ways as well.

Also, keep in mind the "domino effect." Marriage expert Michelle Weiner Davis talks about the positive difference this can make when one spouse decides to change. She writes:

> "I have been working with couples for years and I've learned a lot about how change occurs in relationships. It's like a chain reaction. If one person changes, the other one does too. It's simply a matter of tipping over the first domino. Change is reciprocal."

> - www.divorcebusting.com
> Article, "Why Should I Be the One to Change?"

Working on your own issues can make big and/or small changes, but it does change things. Do what you can and see what happens as a result. Your spouse may or may not change his or her actions, but you never know. It's sure worth the effort. And even so, your doing the right thing is better than neither of you doing it. God notices. That is a great benefit in and of itself.

As I said, the information to make positive changes in conflict issues is out there. I can't go into all the details here. But please start with prayer, asking God to change you and your approaches. And then seek the info you need. A great place to start is on the Marriage Missions website. Go into the "Communication and Conflict" topic, along with the "Communication Tools" topic, and start prayerfully reading, gleaning the info you can use, and then start applying what you learn. We also lead you to a lot of other websites and recommended resources to help as well.

It's one step at a time, inch by inch. But the goal is to inch forward, even if you fall backward sometimes in this journey. Start going through the quotes that we have posted in those two topics, and that should give you a great start as you apply what you learn.

H.A.L.T. Times

I'll share just a few of the many things we've learned that have helped us to re-solve our conflicting situations so both of us are satisfied. One of them is the H.A.L.T. Approach. When you have an important matter you need to work through with your spouse, it is helpful to know when to make your approach. Don't do it during a time when you should H.A.L.T. This would be a time when either of you is Hungry, Angry, Lonely, or Tired. There's more vulnerability to be less tolerant during those times.

> "A number of studies demonstrate that we tend to give people more benefit of the doubt [and grace] when we're in a good mood and less benefit of the doubt when in a bad mood [or one of the above factors is in play]. If you're in a bad mood, you're more likely to perceive whatever your partner says or does more negatively, no matter how positive he or she is trying to be."
>
> - Scott Stanley, Daniel Trathen, Savanna McCain, and Milt Bryan
> "A Lasting Promise: A Christian Guide to Fighting for Your Marriage," p. 53

The point is to ask God to help you to discern when would be the best time to talk with your spouse. You may still get a negative reaction from him or her, but there's less of a chance of it if you pick a better time to make your approach. (We discuss this more in depth on our website.)

In the past, Steve and I would often argue just before bedtime—that was bad timing! Both of us were so upset before trying to go to sleep. Steve would go to sleep (albeit, it wasn't a restful sleep) because that was one of his escapism habits from childhood. But I couldn't sleep. I'd stay up all night stewing.

And trying to stay up to argue the whole matter through didn't work out well either. We were too tired to make wise choices in how we would talk to each other. Plus, we would be wiped out the next day. And still, we didn't really resolve our differences to the point that we both felt satisfied.

So now, when there is a matter that we need to work through and it is in the evening, we concede to visit it at a later agreed upon time. (We keep it away from a "tired" time when we aren't as sharp to talk and truly listen to each other, as we should when we're trying to re-solve our differences.) We then both work to drop the issue from our minds that evening so we don't stew about it all night. That's a bit challenging to do when you are upset about something, but we have both found that it is doable, and it truly is the best way to handle conflict issues. We don't want to sin and allow the sun to go down on our anger (see: Ephesians 4:26), and we don't want to enter into a marathon arguing mode all evening, into the morning—going at it until it's finally resolved. If we're conflicted and it's getting later in the day or evening, we've found that it's best for us to drop it for that time, and then "discuss" it later.

And then if things get too heated when we do revisit the issue, we take another time-out and talk about the matter at another time. That keeps us away from an overly "angry" time when we are volatile to sinning in our anger—something we're told not to do in God's Word. (See: Ephesians 4:26.) This has helped us a lot in coming to places of agreement with each other.

S.T.O.P. Arguing in Front of Others

Another tool we recommend using is the S.T.O.P. guideline in resolving conflict. When you or your spouse is upset over a matter, and you are with other people, do what you can to S.T.O.P. arguing. S.T.O.P.... See The Other People. Be considerate of their wants, not just your impulse to argue it out, no matter who's with you. When you argue with an audience around you, you pull them into your fights. Who wants that? Only dysfunctional people would want to be involved in your arguments (unless there is the threat of abuse, which is a totally different matter that needs to be stopped). Please don't put them in this place. It's rude and unkind to the extreme.

There is a difference between talking through a conflict in respectful ways and fighting in front of others. The first is a judgment call, when you are trying to teach your children how to resolve differences in healthy ways. The second is just plain rude. We've been subjected to this type of behavior between married couples, and it is painful to watch. We've just wanted to run out of the room (and actually have excused ourselves a few times). It is an awkward situation at its best.

Steve and I became aware of the importance of the S.T.O.P. guideline after watching a television program a few years back. It brought this point home to us all the more. This point was aired on a national television program called the Dr. Phil Show. Before it aired, Dr. Phil McGraw had video cameras placed (with their permission) in the home of a married couple. They asked him to help them with the fights they were having with each other. The cameras recorded some of their fights.

Afterward, Dr. Phil had the husband and wife sitting together on his show to watch, with the audience, a part of what was videotaped. It was a very tough program to watch, but important. The video showed the husband and wife screaming at each other vile, destructive things. The children were right there in the room watching and hearing everything that was going on. It was quite evident from the children's behavior that they were extremely conflicted about all that was happening. The daughter was even crying, pleading, and yelling at her parents to stop. The son just sat in stunned silence, rocking back and forth, obviously very disturbed.

But still, this couple continued on as if the children were invisible. And for the most part, the parents admitted later, they were. The parents said they didn't even notice their children's reactions. They were so caught up in their own agendas that they literally stepped over the children to verbally assault each other. They didn't even notice what this was doing to their kids.

When this husband and wife watched the video, they both realized how horrible this was for everyone involved—especially their children. They resolved to find the help they needed to change their behavior from that day forward. With help, they learned how to resolve their conflicts in healthier ways, and also take their arguments away from their children. What a great relief that must be for all involved!

On a personal note, my dad and his wife did this to Steve and me. A number of times, we were riding in the back seat of their car with them, and they were up front bickering as they were driving us to some location. We felt like trapped animals. I'm sure this is how young children feel when they are in a place where they can't escape their parents fighting. Each time I tried to talk to my dad and his wife about the fact that we didn't want to be a part of their fights. They never changed their behavior. So, we decided to change ours.

Fortunately, because we were adults and we had more choices than young children do, we finally told them that we would never ride with them in a car again. We would drive separately. This isn't what we wanted to do, but it was better than the alternative. That way they could fight away, and we could ride in peace. It ended up being a great decision.

I say all of this to plead with you not to subject others to your fights. We've been with friends and relatives who have done this to us. We have had to find ways to escape their rudeness. Please don't subject your friends, relatives, children, or outsiders to your arguments. Keep it private. S.T.O.P. See The Other People, and give them a break!

If Walls Could Talk

How I wish we could put cameras in everyone's home so they could see how dysfunctional some of their arguing gets. We wrote a Marriage Message a while back that brings out the point. It's titled "If Walls Could Talk." If your walls could talk, what do you think they'd say? Oh, we're not talking about the private moments between husband and wife where certain things should be kept private between them and God. We mean over-all, what would they say?

We're told in the Bible in Proverbs 24:3-4, NIV: "By wisdom a house is built, and through understanding it is established. Through knowledge its rooms are filled with rare and beautiful treasures." So, are the rooms of your home being built with wise words of understanding and knowledge of the ways of the Lord? The principles for loving each other are the principles for living, as written throughout the Bible. If the walls of your home could talk, what would they say about how you personally conduct yourself within your marriage relationship?

When you are arguing with your spouse, H.A.L.T., if it is a time when it's not as wise to go into any areas of disagreement. And when you do, S.T.O.P. and See The Other People and take your arguing elsewhere out of their earshot and eyesight. And then do what you can so that wherever and whenever you and your spouse argue, you conduct yourselves with understanding and wisdom. Learn what you need to, so you get to that place. You will never do it all perfectly, but at least lean in that direction.

Slow It Down… Talk and Listen

One last tool (among many) that we often recommend is something called the "Speaker/Listener Technique." This is a tool that has helped us and millions of other couples. It is one that slows down the conflict so you both take turns talking and listening to each other. To truly re-solve conflicts, you need to talk to each other (not at) and also listen to what each of you is trying to communicate. This method embraces giving each other grace and space, and extending respect, so both of you feel heard and better understood.

It's a tool we learned about by taking PREP training. It helps those who are getting married, or are married, to learn the basics of good communication skills. We have a communication tool posted on the Marriage Missions website that explains it better than I can here. And then we have a link posted at the end of the article, which points you to a book that can best explain it.

Basically, it is a method of giving each other turns in (respectfully) talking and then listening to the other speak. In the marriage relationship, one spouse talks and the other spouse listens to what is being said. And then the listening spouse sums up what he or she thought he or she heard. They then switch places and the listening spouse now has the opportunity to talk uninterrupted and the other one listens, reflecting back afterward what he or she thought he or she heard. They go back and forth until both spouses feel they have heard and voiced what needs to be said.

This way both spouses can better get to a place of understanding and work to resolve, to the best of their abilities, the issue at hand. Sometimes they just agree to disagree, but it is a mutual decision. That is an important point—they are mutually deciding. That's what marriage partners do when it comes to important matters of concern.

When some people hear of this technique, they say in their minds, No way could I do this, or would my spouse do this! It seems so formal and restricting, but that's the point.

A few years back we were working with a couple who were continually arguing with each other in very demeaning ways. It was a mess. I told the husband about this method, and he said to me, "There's no way I will do this. I can't express my thoughts as well in this format." I told him that was the reason we were recommending this. He and his wife needed to slow down their thought exchange. Both of them were continually voicing their thoughts in raw, unfiltered, forceful ways, and no one was hearing what the other one was trying to say. They needed to slow things down so they could better think before they said things that they shouldn't.

Here's a point that is important to consider:

> "You may be thinking, 'This sure is artificial.' Agreed. In fact, that's the key reason it is so effective. The truth is, what comes naturally to couples when difficult issues come up is often destructive and quite the opposite from being 'quick to hear, slow to speak, and slow to become angry.' Again, James shows his tendency toward purifying bluntness. 'If anyone considers himself religious and yet does not keep a tight rein on his tongue, he deceives himself and his religion is worthless.'"

- James 1:26
Scott Stanley, Daniel Trathen, Savanna McCain, and Milt Bryan
"A Lasting Promise: A Christian Guide to Fighting for Your Marriage," p. 66

And at that time, this particular husband's and wife's tongues were getting them into trouble. I asked the husband how their present style of arguing was working for them. He admitted that it was bad. She said it was horrible. I then told him that if he and his wife had another way of doing this so it actually worked better, to use it. But if they couldn't, I asked them to try this one.

They refused and never did. They just kept doing what they had been done in the past, expecting different results (the definition of insanity). Eventually, they got a divorce. Their arguing was so toxic that it took down their marriage. It absolutely breaks our hearts to think about this couple. They are completely closed to trying to reconcile their marriage. It didn't have to be. They both are good people who love the Lord. How this must especially break the Lord's heart!

So, if you are destructive in how you argue with each other concerning conflicting matters, please look into trying this technique. Steve and I have used it. And now, we are able to work through our conflicts without really "formally" using this technique. It is now ingrained in how we interact with each other. This helps us to talk, listen, and reflect back what we think we hear the other person is saying, so there is now more clarity in understanding the bigger picture. From this stance, we can better work on solutions that both of us feel works for us.

Beware of Blurting

Just because something comes into your mind, it doesn't mean that you should say it. (The married couple we just talked about is a prime example of this problem.) Beware of blurting out whatever first comes to mind if it is not "wholesome talk." (See Ephesians 4:29.) Biting your tongue and holding back certain thoughts—running them past the Lord first before blurting them out in all of their rawness—is wise. There is wisdom in pausing first before speaking.

There is a false notion going around that "a great relationship lets you vent all your feelings." That is totally not true. A marriage license does not give you the license or permission to blurt out whatever you want to say whenever you want to say it. Marriage partners need to be smarter than that. That is how you can destroy your relationship, not grow it.

God tells us in Proverbs 29:11, ESV: "A fool gives full vent to his spirit, but a wise man [or woman] quietly holds it back." Speak words motivated by love, rather than vindictiveness. Talk; don't blurt. Don't dump all of your emotional garbage onto your spouse.

> "Ask the Lord to put a 'governor' on your tongue today, to enable you to speak only words that reflect the heart of Christ. If you feel the need to 'vent' tell the Lord what's on your mind, rather than blurting it out to your spouse."
>
> - Nancy Leigh DeMoss
> "The Quiet Place: Daily Devotional Readings," April 19

It's like what Dr. Phil McGraw says:

> "Getting things off your chest might feel good, but when you blurt something out in the heat of the moment, you risk damaging your relationship permanently. Many relationships are destroyed when one partner can't forgive something that was said during uncensored venting. But before you say something you might regret, bite your tongue and give yourself a moment to consider how you really feel. The things we say while we're letting loose often don't represent how we really feel and shouldn't be communicated—especially if they are potentially destructive."
>
> - Dr. Phil McGraw
> "Love Smart"

Plus, this confirms all the more what God tells us in the Bible in Ecclesiastes 10:12-13, NIV: "Words from a wise man's mouth are gracious, but a fool is consumed by his own lips. At the beginning his words are folly; at the end they are wicked madness—and the fool multiplies words." Did you see that? It says, "At the beginning his words are folly . . ." and "at the end they are wicked madness." In other words, if you begin to blurt out folly, you will end with "wicked madness." Further in Scripture we're told:

> "Do not be quick with your mouth, do not be hasty in your heart to utter anything before God. God is in heaven and you are on earth, so let your words be few."
>
> - Ecclesiastes 5:2
> NIV

> "Do you see a man who speaks in haste? There is more hope for a fool than for him."
>
> - Proverbs 29:20
> NIV

> "If anyone considers himself religious and yet does not keep a tight rein on his tongue, he deceives himself and his religion is worthless."
>
> - James 1:26
> NIV

This is so very true. I ran across the following very wise words:

"Practice the pause.

When in doubt, pause.

When angry, pause.

When tired, pause.

When stressed, pause.

And when you pause, pray."

- Unknown

Two ways you can "practice the pause" is by using the H.A.L.T. Method, and the S.T.O.P. guideline, along with taking a breath to pause before you speak. Slow it down, and be aware that not only does your spouse hear the garbage you dump out, if you don't put a governor on your tongue, but God does too. Ask yourself, "Would I say this if I could literally see my pastor, or more importantly, Jesus in the room receiving these words?" It might slow you down.

Keep in mind that sometimes we slam our spouse's ears shut from listening to even the good stuff when we dump out the bad stuff in the heat of the moment. Choose your words wisely.

> "Our abrasive words can cut off hearing, just as Peter's sword cut off the servant's ear. We just can't come against people whenever we feel like justice is needed. We must be submissive to God."
>
> - Joyce Meyer,
> "Making Marriage Work"

Bite your tongue rather than blurting out whatever first comes to your mind. And if you do:

> "If you have played the fool and exalted yourself, or if you have planned evil, clap your hand over your mouth! For as churning the milk produces butter, and as twisting the nose produces blood, so stirring up anger produces strife."
>
> - Proverbs 30:32-33

NIV

Don't exalt yourself into thinking that your opinion needs to be shoved out there—whether it's a foolish one or not. But if you do give it, be wise enough to go to your spouse and in humility, confess your sin (because that's what it is if it is mean-spirited, lacking love and consideration). And then ask for forgiveness.

Marriage Essential #6
Stand United:
Don't Let Family, Friends, or Things Separate You

There was a very popular song released in 1970 called "United We Stand." The chorus said:

"For united we stand; / Divided we fall. / And if our backs should ever be against the wall / We'll be together, together, you and I."

- Tony Hiller
"Brotherhood of Man"

Far too often we see couples not standing united in their marriages, and when their backs are against the wall they divide. In this essential we hope to show you the incredible strength you will have when you commit to standing united in your relationship.

Cindy

Standing united is easier before you marry, plus when you are standing at the altar gazing into each other's idealistic eyes. But it takes more than idealism and the memory of a fun wedding to help you to stand united when life starts invading your "world of two." It takes tenacity and steadfast commitment.

A while back I wrote an Insight titled "Stubbornly Married." I wrote it because that's something Steve and I have had to do in our marriage. If we weren't stubbornly married, we would have called it quits years ago. It's kind of like the wife who told her husband, "If you leave me, I'm going with you." It takes that kind of tenacity and stubbornness to stay married when it seems like everyone around you is dumping out of marriage. I also wrote on the subject of being stubbornly married because God impressed upon me that unless we are stubborn in not allowing anyone or anything else to divide us, it too easily happens.

We live in a world that is obsessed with falling in love and marrying "our soul mate." But our society in large is not good at supporting those who find that special type of love. "Leave him or her"... "dump him or her and start over with a clean slate" is advice we hear repeatedly. But that's not God's approach—that's man's. God's approach to marriage is all about persevering and working through our issues—not leaving and forsaking. Being stubbornly married is what God asks of us when we say, "I do." Those are serious words to Him, and they need to be to us as well.

When you think of the term stubbornly married, what comes to mind? To us it means digging in and not letting anyone or anything separate you. It's a matter of remembering Jesus' words when He said, "What God has put together, let no man separate." There is an abundance of people and things that can separate us in our marriages. And that can include us. We can give up and allow our minds and actions to go in directions they shouldn't. I agree with something Kelsey Robertson wrote on this issue:

"Love needs to be stubborn. Love is not always easy, so the key to real love is being too stubborn to let it ever go away. If you do not stubbornly insist on loving your spouse, then it is easy for that love to slip away. Love must be stubborn to survive."

- www.familyshare.com
Article, "10 Things You Didn't Realize About Love Until After Marriage"

Are you stubbornly married? Or are you finding yourself slipping away from the closeness you should have as husband and wife?

I'm going to give you a few examples of the different people and things that can cause a division between us in our marriage. For one, we can allow other people to cause a divide between us.

This can be our parents, relatives, friends, coworkers, and even our children. When we give more of our time, and priority to them, it means we give our spouse the leftovers. You know, we didn't make a vow to any of them on our wedding day. God didn't tell us to cleave to any of them. He told a husband and wife to do this. So, we must take heed.

Some of the people who can divide us are friends and coworkers. We already talked about this in another Marriage Essential. But I want to make one more point, concerning our friends and how we have to make sure they don't cause separation between us, as husband and wife.

Friends Who Cause Division in Your Marriage

A person might say that if they let go of this friend, they "won't have any friends." That could be true, but, in reality, it would be better to not have any friends for a season, even a long one, than to have friends who pull you in a wrong direction. It's the Matthew 5:29-30 principle that if your "hand" or your "eye" causes you to do what you shouldn't, then you must get rid of the source of the problem. Friendships can be disposable, but marriages are not supposed to be. It's important to stay true to the vows we made to our God and to our spouse.

When you have to let go of a friend:

> "Understand that you have not lost your friend, but that the conditions of your friendship have changed. The relationship

between a husband and wife should be the most intimate and important relationship experienced by human beings. It takes precedence over friendships and even other family members. That is how God instituted marriage and all should respect that fact."

Lee Wilson
www.crosswalk.com
Article, "My Best Friend's Marriage"

Watch the friendships you keep. Some friendships can be, or grow to be, toxic to your marriage partnership. When you marry, you are to give up your "single-minded" lifestyle.

I can't emphasize enough the importance of God's Word, where Jesus said, "What God has joined together, let no man [or woman] separate" (Matthew 19:6; Mark 10:9, NIV). No one and no thing should be allowed to cause separation between you. That includes no friendships (including Internet "friends" who can invade your marital world), relatives, work, recreation, household responsibilities, material stuff, and the list goes on.

Pushy Parents and Family Members

This leads to the next point, as far as people who can push you and your spouse apart, and that includes parents and other family members. I want to say here that we have a lot of articles and quotes from marriage experts posted on the Marriage Missions website that can put all of this in perspective as far as the husband and wife standing united. They are posted in the "Dealing with In-Laws and Parents" topic. It will give you a much broader perspective of how to stand united and still honor and show your parents love.

Briefly, though, I want to say that we are told to be respectful to parents, but not to cleave to them after we marry. Yes, we are to be reasonably attentive to them and to others. But if we allow them to cause an emotional and/or physical separation, we are violating our promises to God and to our spouse. It's important to be stubbornly committed to our marriage and NOT to allow this separation because of unhealthy relationships with others. Remember what we're told in the Bible:

"For this reason, a man will leave his father and mother and be united to his wife, and the two will become one flesh. So they are no longer two but one. Therefore what God has joined together, let man not separate."

- Mark 10:7-8
NIV

Think also of the "cord of three strands" referred to in Ecclesiastes 4:12. We believe the three strands include the husband, wife, and God alone. God didn't include four, five six, or seven strands to include other family members. God said the three strands, intertwined together, are "not quickly broken." You would think additional strands would make that cord even stronger. But God doesn't see it that way. He knows the dynamics of the bridegroom and bride, with Him wrapping them up in His care. Other strands can cause separation if they are included. It's okay if they are on the outside looking in—supporting from that stance. But they are not to be a part of that primary marital bond.

It's a lot like what Sydney Smith said:

> "Marriage is to resemble a pair of shears, so joined that they cannot be separated, often moving in opposite directions, yet always punishing anyone who comes between them."

We've had to apply these principles in our own marriage several times. Steve talks about this in his portion of this essential. But I've had to apply this essential in our marriage as well. Earlier in our marriage, I had to stop my mom at one point and let her know that I was not married to her, but to Steve. She tried to order me to do something her way. I knew that this was a "drawing a line in the sand" time when I had to say no to her demands. She could no longer try to tell me what to do. My marriage to Steve changed her authority over me.

Yes, I told her she could suggest things to me. And I told her I would listen and pray about it. I let her know that I respected her opinion and loved her, but the dynamic of the mother/daughter relationship changed after my marriage to Steve. It really hurt her at first when this happened. And I was scared that it would permanently scar our relationship. Fortunately, this confrontation actually helped our relationship, rather than hurt it. My mom never tried ordering me around after that. And she never tried to step over Steve to interfere in our marriage in ways she shouldn't have.

But even if it didn't go in that positive direction, I still had to take the chance to say something to her when boundaries were being violated. Marriage brings into the picture the need to put up some guidelines if family members or friends are causing division between the spouses. If they are cheerleaders who encourage the married couple... great! And if they are advisers, and give good counsel (not demands)... great! But if they are trying to exert authority, then it's important to nip that in the bud, to the best of your ability.

Even if you've been married for a while, you can still do this. It's better to stop a harmful action from continuing than to let it go on and on just because you have let it happen up to this point.

Time Spent with Extended Family

It may even be that the parents aren't overtly causing division between you. They may be very respectful and honor your marriage unity. But it may be the amount of time you are spending with parents that are causing problems. If you and your spouse both agree on spending a lot of time with one or both sets of parents and/or siblings, then great! You are standing united. But if one spouse complains that he or she is feeling crowded and needs less time spent with extended family and more time spent one-on-one, or even just together with your kids, then this needs to be heeded.

Sara Horn gives great advice on this:

> "Plan space in your schedule and treat it as sacred. There's nothing wrong with spending time with family. But if you're at your parents' home more than you are your own [and one spouse feels it's too much], it's time to reexamine priorities. Sit down with your spouse and a calendar and decide what nights and weeks are reserved just for the two of you and your children, if you have them. Then treat those times as sacred for just each other."

- www.crosswalk.com
Article, "5 Ways to Give Your Marriage the Attention It Deserves"

The Cultural Divide

There is also a cultural matter that needs to be addressed here. There are many cultures, communities, and individual families where the parents are given too much authority to interfere in their grown kids' marriages. I understand that this makes it all the more difficult to set up necessary boundaries with families. This is the way that culture (or family) has always approached these matters. Many cultures allow parents and in-laws to boss around their married "kids." That means that you will be judged by, not only your parents, if you do things differently, but also by many, many other people in the community. And that's a difficult force with which to reckon.

But when a culture goes against a Biblical principle, then you need to go the way of what God tells you rather than the culture. In Noah's day, everyone else was sinning and doing things they shouldn't. It looked as though Noah was the fool when he didn't go the way of his community. But after the rain started, who looked like the fools? Everyone else was doing things a different way than Noah and his family, but everyone else was wrong. We are to go God's way, not man's way.

From the Perspective of a Child

I'll never forget when our young grandson told me to tell his dad (my son) to stop doing something that he did not like. I told my grandson that I couldn't do that. I told him that I had already talked to his dad about that, and now it's up to him to decide what he would do from there. My grandson said, "Well, make him do it; you're his mom!" I just laughed and said, "That ship sailed a long time ago when he started living on his own, paying his own bills, and especially after he got married. I can't tell him what to do any longer (nor should I)."

I told him that because his dad is married to his mom, my job is now to be their encouragers—not a parent who tells them what to do. My grandson then said, "Okay then, encourage my dad not to (fill in the blank)." He sure didn't get it that I was no longer the authority figure in his dad's life just because I'm his mom. This is a difficult concept for a six-year-old to grasp.

But apparently, it's a difficult thing for many grown "kids" and/or their parents to grasp as well. I can't even start to tell you the number of times we're contacted about this very dividing matter. These spouses want us to do something about it. We can't. All we can do is tell them what the Bible says. It's up to them to do what it takes so it is lived out in their marriage to the best of their ability. And that is definitely easier said than done. But isn't that true of every relationship issue?

Living with Parents or Vice Versa

Even if the grown "kids" decide to live with their parent(s), or the parent(s) live with them, that boundary still needs to be put into place. The parents are their own main family unit, and their grown married kids are their own main family unit too. The parents are not to push themselves into that dynamic. If it's not lived out, then some adjustments need to be made. It isn't to be made to the marriage, but to the live-in arrangements. Relationship boundaries must be put into place, or God's plan is not being honored as it should be, and that becomes very troublesome.

Most often, it works out best if parents and their married kids don't live together. They may do fine if they live next door to each other, but if not, then they may need to put even more distance between them. Clearer boundaries can be put in place when they live separately. Sometimes, it is even necessary to put geographical distance between them. But if that isn't possible, then make sure everyone honors the marriage priority of a husband and wife standing united.

I want to say here that if the husband's family is interfering in his marriage, then he should be the spokesperson to set his family straight. Even if the tension is going on between two females (his mom or sister and his wife), this should still be the rule. It is his family member, and he needs to stick up for his wife (or talk to his wife about his family member, if she is at fault). This is a very uncomfortable situation, especially for most men. They have a tendency to back away from two fighting females—understandably so. But following the Biblical principle of honoring his wife as first priority is how it should be, even if he must point out something that she needs to correct. No matter what the issue is, he should talk on her behalf and in her defense when there are family relationship problems that arise from his in-laws or her interaction with them. And he should not talk in demeaning ways about his spouse. His mission is to build a bridge, not a wall, whenever it is possible. He should be firm and kind in how he approaches the matter.

And if it is the wife's family that is causing problems, the same principle applies. She is to be the main spokesperson for and to her family member(s). Our own family members will have the tendency to give us a lot more grace and forgiveness than they will from an "in-law."

Parent/Child Emotional Bonding

Another point I want to touch on is when parents get their primary emotional needs met through their married son or daughter. Or maybe the son or daughter was tied to the parent before marriage and is still continuing on in the same way after marriage. Honestly, this needs to change. This is a huge threat to the closeness that marital partners should have with each other.

Counselor and author Sandra Lundberg wrote:

> "If your spouse gets his or her emotional needs met in his or her relationship with parents instead of with you, there's a problem. You may even feel as if your spouse is having an affair. Sometimes this problem begins when a wife feels frustrated over her husband's seeming lack of interest in conversing about her day. She starts talking with her parents instead. Sometimes the husband is the frustrated one. It's common for mother and son to have long or frequent conversations that leave the wife feeling ignored. Neither scenario is appropriate. Respect for each other is the key. In this situation, respect might require that the spouse maintaining an overly close relationship with his or her parents will decrease that contact in order to show love for the spouse.
>
> "...This is not to suggest that children and parents should cut off their relationship under the guise of leaving and cleaving. But your primary human relationship now is with your spouse, not your parents."
>
> - "The First Five Years of Marriage," p. 317

Point made!

Children Can Separate You

I want to make one last point on the people who can cause separation between a husband and wife. Our own children can cause division and separateness. As cute and as needy as they are, it's important that we don't go overboard in caring for them to the degree that we neglect our marital relationship.

> "One of the big struggles with marriage today is the tendency to put our kids' needs before those of our spouse. What we don't realize is that child-centered marriages are often weak marriages. And in the long run they hurt the kids more than help them. If your spouse is not getting his or her emotional needs met by you, often he or she will pour all their energy into the children. The end result is an unhealthy marriage relationship. Obviously, I'm not talking about neglecting your children. I just want to emphasize the importance of seeking to keep your marriage vows a major priority."
>
> - Jim Burns
> "Creating an Intimate Marriage," p. 16

That's so true. We should never allow our children's wants take precedence over our spouse's needs. This is something that moms especially struggle with, although there are some dads who wrestle with this issue as well. Sometimes, it's because they perceive that their wife spends too much time with the kids, and in other cases, it's the dad who invests an overload of time.

One of the hottest articles on the Marriage Missions website deals with "When the Wife Puts the Children Ahead of the Husband." There are husbands who are complaining, and there are wives who are complaining. And then there are comments from both sexes that are defending their stands on this area of parenting and marriage. It's very problematic.

Being a mom, I can easily see how we could spend every waking hour tending to our children's needs. And mostly, they seem like needs, rather than demands. But thankfully, God showed us a long time ago to be careful of not overdoing this to the point that we are neglecting our marriage.

Actually, it's a good thing we nurtured our friendship with each other as a married couple because at this point in our lives, both of our sons are living long distances from us. One is living on the other side of the country, and the other is living on the other side of the world. We would be in horrible shape if we had been a child-centered marriage, at the neglect of our own relationship.

Parent Coaching Consultant Teresa Parr wrote the following as a warning to couples:

> "Babies are loud about what they need. Marriages are not. It's easy to neglect each other because other things are more urgent, but you have to save some time and energy for your spouse."
>
> - Richmond Parents Monthly publication, April 1, 2003
> Article, "Marriage: It's the Little Things That Matter the Most"

And that's what we see and have discovered for ourselves. That which is loud does not necessarily need our primary attention. Sometimes yes... it is necessary to give it. But other times it's better to let the child have some of his or her needs and wants NOT tended to (at least not right away). God doesn't instantly tend to our every need and want. And He certainly makes us wait lots of times when He does give us what we need (or want). Ultimately, it develops our character when we are forced to be patient. The same is true of our children.

> "If you are always pushing your spouse aside for time with the children, you may want to consider just what you're teaching your children. By the way you treat your spouse, are you modeling for your children how you hope they will treat their future spouses? Probably not. Spending time with your spouse not only draws the two of you closer together, but it also teaches your children that the marital relationship has to be our number one human relationship."
>
> - Dr. Debbie L. Cherry
> "Child-Proofing Your Marriage"

There are a lot of grown children and spouses in our world who sure would have benefited from having to wait for some things. When a child is sent the message that they are the center of the universe, it can cause all kinds of problems. Feeling entitled is one of them. And also, divorce is another problem, as the neglected spouse says, "Enough is enough. I need attention, too."

Claudia Arp made this true statement:

> "Your kids will wait while you grab a few moments to build your marriage; but your marriage won't wait until your kids grow up."

Please pay attention to the message of what Claudia is saying here. We are seeing daily, in our ministry, the harmful effects of spouses who have been or are being neglected. Tend to the children's needs… yes, but don't forget to tend to the needs of the marriage either. You didn't marry your children; you married and made promises of love to your spouse.

A Biggie

And here's a biggie that we see separates couples more than we can emphasize: that is past abuse. Of course, present abuse is more than a biggie in separating you. So that needs to be addressed. Abuse from a husband or abuse from a wife (we see both) is absolutely wrong. Abuse always separates; it never brings together. So that must be addressed if it is occurring. We have a lot of articles posted on the Marriage Missions website that give direction on that matter. They are posted in the "Abuse in Marriage" topic. Please take advantage of what we offer.

But in this marriage essential, I'm talking about abuse from a spouse's past that comes up and bites them once again. I'm not sure why, but for some reason, more often than not, past abuse issues go into an almost dormant stage where it looks as if they no longer have a hold on the victim while the couple is dating. But then, at some point after marrying, it comes back to attack like a sleeping dragon that is now more powerful than ever imagined possible.

That's what happened to me, as I have stated previously, and I have talked to hundreds of other victims (mostly women, but some are men) whose past has come back up to haunt them big time. And when that happens, the victimized spouse once again falls victim to the actions of what some monster(s) forced upon them. As I said before, it doesn't stop there (which is horribly sad in itself). But then the other spouse becomes a victim too, and often the children become victims as well when their parents' marriage goes in a dysfunctional direction. Many marriages are broken apart because of past abuse issues. And when that happens, the ripple effects and tidal wave damage can go on for generations.

I mention that the other spouse and children become additional victims as well. That is because it deeply affects their lives just as shrapnel causes additional damage to those who are near any explosion. They don't deserve the bomb dropped on them either.

The monster(s) who committed the original abuse has a tendency to take down numerous innocent victims because of their selfish, self-satisfying behavior. And if we let it, the damage will keep spreading.

My Ah-Ha Moment

I want to explain a bit more of my story because I think it may help others who have been victimized. I remember one day, standing in our kitchen when it hit me, when I decided I couldn't live like this anymore. This wasn't really living—I was just existing, and dragging my damaged carcass through life. I was at the edge of my limits. The nightmares, the haunting memories, and the continual pushing away of my wonderful husband had to stop. I knew this would be the end of me if I didn't proactively do something about it.

So I did. I pleaded with God and asked Him to please take this away. I had done this hundreds, perhaps thousands, of times before, but this time it was different. I knew that I would have to quit allowing this nightmarish occurrence to keep happening, and start doing something that would change this pattern and eliminate it. I told God that I would do anything to make it all stop. And I meant every word of that prayer. Enough was enough!

As soon as I prayed that, I heard the words in my mind, "Do you really want to be healed?" To that I responded, "Yes, I will do anything that is required of me." And then I heard the following strange phrase, "Then hang on, sister; this is going to be a rough journey!" Honestly, I didn't care. It didn't seem that it could be much tougher than what I had already been going through.

I then came to the knowledge that I had to open my eyes, ears, and heart. I knew that God would be working with me on this, as my "Wonderful

Counselor," to help me process through the difficult issues that needed to be dealt with in order to reach a place of healing. And that's just what God did. It seemed like every time I turned around I came across something that would bring to the surface a remembrance of what happened. I would then deal with it in the way I knew I should (and that is a miracle in itself), and then soon the next remembrance would come to mind. Sometimes, it was through something I would read, or something that was said by someone, or a television or radio program, etc. I never knew what would trigger the next step I would take towards healing.

And sometimes it was more painful than I could ever express. But it's kind of like having surgery. You are in a lot of pain before surgery, and then afterward, you are in a lot more pain. But what procedures were done to you in that time of surgery eventually bring lasting relief. And that's what happened. There were bursts of pain, but they lessened and lessened as the abuse issues were dealt with and put away properly. I got to the place where I knew I needed a counselor to help with the rest, and through a long trail of events, I found one who helped me clean up the rest of the mess.

All of this was the most painful journey I could ever describe. But I can't even begin to tell you how glad I am that I took it. Freedom is so sweet. It is sweet to me and it is sweet to my husband. In the midst of all I was going through, God opened my eyes to see that Steve didn't deserve to be another victim of the monsters that hurt me. I had to stop this victimization from growing. I also had to be willing to let go, forgive, and move on in my life—no longer living as a victim but as someone who was released from a prison I was thrown into and didn't deserve.

I am so thankful to be free and thankful that the victimization has ended—for me and for Steve.

Reason for Sharing

There is a reason I am sharing this. It isn't for the reason of writing about me, but to wake up spouses who are living in this type of torture chamber. It is separating them from embracing their spouse in the wonderful way God intends. Abuse hurts; it victimizes; it separates; and it gives the enemy of our faith a victory that should never happen. As we put our hand into God's, He can lead us to victory. It may start out on a rocky road, but it leads to freedom and sweet release.

If you are a victim of abuse—any type of abuse (physical, verbal, sexual, financial, spiritual, or whatever), or if your spouse is a victim of abuse, please, please get help. First, if you have been abused, please reach out for the help you can get for the hurt that has been inflicted upon you. Yes, it will be painful, but in the end, you will be eliminating current and future pain. Make this a mission in your life and your marriage—to get to a healthy, loving, and healing place. Don't give your abuser(s) any more energy or power in your life to torture you. You may need a marriage-friendly counselor to help you in this mission. You want to make sure your marriage survives the healing process. A good counselor will keep your marriage in mind as he or she works with you. Not all counselors do this; so be careful in your selection of the one who will work with you.

If your spouse has been hurt by abuse, you also have a very tough road ahead of you to traverse. You can't make your spouse reach out for healing, but you can get help for yourself to learn how to be the spouse your husband or wife needs. And in the process, you will learn how to be the person you are prodded by God to be. Sometimes you need to embrace, listen to, and hold your spouse, and other times you are to lovingly prod your spouse into a healthier place. It takes godly discernment to know what you are to do when.

Love sometimes comes and is given in soft, tender ways, as in a whisper. I'm thinking of Elijah and how God came to him in a whisper. (See 1 Kings 19:11-12.) And at other times love is given in tough ways. It's the iron sharpening iron process that we're told about in Proverbs 27:17. But it's important to discern what is needed when—especially when you are dealing with someone who has been abused.

One last time... don't let past abuse separate you from your marriage partner. Reach out for help, and keep pursuing healing until it occurs.

THINGS That Separate Spouses

This is another area of married life that overlaps with other essentials that we've given (and we will be giving). But it also stands on its own. In today's world, it's not too difficult to allow other things to cause a separation between our spouse and us. This can include a long line of "things." We're talking about cars, boats, houses, hobbies, and, yes, media. There are a growing number of divorces that are taking place because of Facebook hookups.

And that doesn't even start to go into the other types of digital devices that we allow to invade the space that should be reserved for our spouse. Have you gone into a restaurant lately (especially fast-food ones) and looked around at the people sitting around you? Everywhere you go people have their faces buried in their phones. And when they come home, they have other electronic devices they can include in how they spend their time.

Steve and I went to South Korea to spend time with our adult kids and grandchildren. I remember (more than once) looking around as we were riding the subway. No one, and I literally mean no one, was engaged in conversation, except on his or her phones. Married couples were sitting together with the husband on his phone and his wife on hers. Or one was on his or her phone and the other was looking down. I'm sure if we were riding on a subway train in an American city, or in another country, we would see the same thing.

Why is it that we can't seem to talk to the person next to us and, instead "talk" to someone on a phone? I remember wanting to scream out, "People, pay attention to the one you're with. Do that in private!" I wanted to do that, but I'm sure it wouldn't have gone over very well. I would have just been pegged as a crazy person, and I would have embarrassed my family. But who's truly crazy here?

We need to wake up. Technology is great. I'm all for it. But just as it is with anything, you need to be balanced in how much time you spend on it. It's important not to allow it to invade your married life to the point that you spend more time with your phone or computer than you do with your spouse. These devices, and the time we allow ourselves to spend on them, can be time zappers.

There are other ways we allow "creeping separateness" to take over the amount of time and energy we give to our spouse. That's when other things and priorities take over what we should save for our spouse. That sure wasn't included in the vow we made to our spouse, or the vow they made to us. We ALL need to remember that... us too. We aren't immune to letting other things shove us in the wrong direction. And when it happens, it's important to realign our priorities. It's like what Dr Steve

Stephens wrote:

> "It's a sad state of affairs when we take better care of our cars and houses than we do our marriages. We change the oil, fill the tank, check the tires, and periodically tune up our cars. We change light bulbs, wash windows, paint walls, unplug toilets, and re-roof our houses, but what do we do to maintain our marriage? The truth is... more damage is done than repairs are made. How important is your marriage? Is it more important to you than your car or your home? Are you willing to put in the time, energy and whatever else it takes to prove to your partner how valuable the relationship truly is to you?"
>
> - Dr. Steve Stephens
> "Marriage: Experiencing The Best," p. 12

TRAGEDIES Can Separate Us

And lastly, on this marriage essential of standing united, don't allow tragedies to separate you as a married couple. Many times couples don't even realize it's happening. Other times they do, but they don't know how to steer it in a better direction. All they're trying to do at the moment is survive themselves, let alone help the marriage to survive.

These tragedies can include losing a job, a house, bankruptcy, a prodigal or mentally ill child, miscarriages, a rape or attack, or it can be the death or chronic illness of a loved one that causes us to look away from our spouse. The list can go on. We don't understand our spouse's actions or reactions, so we let toxic thinking creep in and push our spouse away for us. It's during those times that we especially need to sink into the commitment of being stubbornly married.

The enemy of our faith delights in taking advantage of times of confusion and hurt. Don't give up that foothold. Turn towards each other and vow not to give in or give up.

The point we're trying to make is to choose to make it through your trials together. As musician Steven Curtis Chapman said to his wife after the horrible death of their five-year-old daughter Marie:

> "This is going to be hard. But we're going to make it. We will find a way to make it together."

He said this to his wife and his family, looking to God to help him/them to do so. And this is what we challenge you to do. Don't let tribulations and differences split you apart. Trials will come. It rains on the good and the evil alike. (See Matthew 5:45.) But determine with God's help, "We will make it together."

It's like what Dr Neal Clark Warren said:

> "When two people cling to each other in a crisis and pour out their feelings to a God they both trust and love, there is a merging and blending that weaves them together at their deepest levels."

Steve and I have found this to be true in our own lives. When Steve was diagnosed with Type-1 Diabetes early in our marriage, our whole world turned upside down. Anyone who lives with diabetes—whether you are a diabetic or you live with a spouse who has it—you know it changes everything. Life delivers its own uncertainties anyway, but when diabetes comes into the picture, it's all up for grabs. It's the number one cause of blindness, heart disease, kidney failure, and the list goes on and on. You aren't sure you will ever have the luxury of making long-term plans. As a matter of fact, I was told by one of Steve's doctors that I would be a young widow raising our two young sons on my own. This was a real eye-opener for me and for Steve.

As a result, despite the many, many challenges thrown at us by life (especially Steve's diabetes and now the heart issues), we have dug in with all the more determination than ever to enjoy the simple things of life. As they say, "Each day is a gift. That is why it is called the present." With God's leading, we don't make many long-term plans. We mostly enjoy each day as it comes. And that is with determination.

We never know when saying, "I love you," if it will be our last time speaking those words to each other on this side of heaven. We learned that a while back when Steve had the widow-maker heart attack. Praise God, Steve is doing great. No one would even guess this happened if they didn't know our personal journey together. He's as active as ever. But with the damage this heart attack caused to his heart, we're all the more aware that each day is a gift. We pray that we embrace our "present" and spend it wisely.

I pray that for you too. Even if you aren't dealing with diabetes or other health issues, job losses, car crashes, accidents, family conflicts, illnesses, or the death of loved ones, etc., please don't take each other for granted. You never know what life will push at you a few minutes from now. Don't let people, things, or life's difficulties separate you. Lean in towards each other; don't lean out and away from each other. We have an article posted on the Marriage Missions website that I recommend you read. It explains a bit about the "cocooning method" of leaning in so you weather the difficulties. The article is titled "When Winds of Adversity Blow." It can be found in the "Marriage Insights" topic. Please read it; I believe it could help you so you are better prepared for those times in your marriage.

Whatever you do, make it your mission to try to work through any tragic issues you have gone through in your life so it doesn't separate you. And give each other the grace and space you each need during tragic times. Even so, to the best of your ability, lean in towards each other, to be there in support whenever you can.

May the Lord help you in this mission in your marriage partnership! "May the Lord direct your hearts into God's love and Christ's perseverance" (2 Thessalonians 3:5, NIV).

Ask God for wisdom to learn whatever you need to overcome relationship obstacles that come before you. Be stubborn in doing whatever it takes to be the spouse God wants you to be. Stubbornly hold on to God and on to each other. That's what it is to be stubbornly married—to stand united.

STEVE

In this essential, Cindy and I touch on a few of the same points. We feel we each bring a different perspective from which you can learn a lot.

When we say to stand united, often what comes to my mind is a military application. I recently read the book Flags of Our Fathers, the account of the battle for Iwo Jima in WW II. Seventy thousand U.S. Marines battled eighteen thousand Japanese soldiers for thirty-six days before claiming victory. The loss of life and the number injured were astronomical on both sides. Every marine who set foot on that island knew the theory of why he was there—he was fighting for his country. But that's not what brought the victory. What motivated each man was that he knew he was there to fight to save the life of the man (his brother) standing next to him... even if it cost him his own life. They stood united to the death.

Oh how Cindy and I wish we could convey to you, and every couple, how important it is for you to have the same mentality and commitment to stand united in your marriage (to the death). So, no matter what attacks you experience from the outside (or the inside) you can defeat that enemy.

We've already talked extensively about the internal things/enemies that can destroy your marriage. These are things like anger, jealousy, abuse, and sexual sin. We've also talked about what you can do to protect yourselves from those. Now we need to address some of the more external enemies that can attack and destroy your marriage.

Here's a great description of what standing united means:

> "Standing united in everything makes a strong marriage. Always show others that you are on your spouse's side. Your spouse is a part of you and you are a part of your spouse. Don't let anyone or anything come between the two of you. Standing united keeps others from penetrating the fragile walls that protect your marriage."
>
> - Shirley Lee Cooper
> www.Americanmarriageministryblogspot.com
> Article, "Standing United"

Of course, the strongest admonition for standing united in marriage comes from the Bible. Here's a great summation from Wikipedia:

> "In Mark 3:25, 'And if a house be divided against itself, that house cannot stand.' Similar verses of the New Testament include Matthew 12:25, 'And Jesus knew their thoughts, and said unto them, every kingdom divided against itself is brought to desolation; and every city or house divided against itself shall not stand.' And Luke 11:17 reiterates, 'But he, knowing their thoughts, said unto them, every kingdom divided against itself is brought to desolation; and a house divided against a house falleth.'"

That should eliminate any questions on the high priority God places on standing united as a couple.

Unity Starts by Leaving and Cleaving?

In more than twenty-five years of marriage ministry, Cindy and I have heard from multiple thousands who have lamented about how one spouse puts someone or something ahead of him or her. The most common problem is when a husband or wife places a higher priority on their family of origin over their spouse. This can be an unhealthy loyalty to a mother, father, sister or brother.

This is why when Cindy and I counsel/mentor an engaged couple, one of the questions we ask is "What is the relationship like between your future husband/wife and their family?" We try to drill down to make sure there are no unhealthy familial attachments before they get married. That's because if they aren't committed to the "leave and cleave" principle before they get married, it's not likely they will honor it after they are married. At least not without a lot of conflict.

As a quick refresher on what the Bible says about this:

> "Therefore a man shall leave his father and his mother and hold fast to his wife, and they shall become one flesh."
>
> - Genesis 2:24
> ESV

And...

> "Then, Jesus said, 'For this reason a man will leave his father and mother and be united to his wife, and the two will become one flesh'? So they are no longer two, but one flesh. Therefore what God has joined together, let man not separate.'"
>
> - Mark 10:8-9,
ESV

I don't want it to escape your attention that God places the bulk of responsibility on the husband to make sure the relationship between him and his wife takes precedence over all other relationships.

Relating to these verses, commentator John Kess said,

> "Despite men and women having completely equal value and worth, God has given different responsibilities to men than He has to women and vice versa. One of the responsibilities that God has assigned to men is to take the initiative in his relationship with his wife (or in the case of a premarital relationship, the woman he desires to be his wife). When God says that 'man shall leave his father and his mother and hold fast to his wife,' He is implicitly telling men to take the initiative in the relationship."

> "...Complementarian theology, if correctly understood, does not make women inferior to men in the least. Rather, it is a call to men and to women to live out the responsibilities that God has given each of them."

- John Kess,
Johnkess.wordpress.com
Article, "Does a Woman Leave Her Parents and Cleave to Her Husband?"

As I was doing research on this topic, I came across one divorce attorney's blog that highlights the disastrous results of not leaving and cleaving. She wrote to caution women about marrying a man who has an "unhealthy" relationship with his mother:

> "For women who fall in love with a son who is attached to his mother, it is difficult to provide any firm advice. However, if the son is always putting the mother first and obeys every

command without question, then it is unlikely he will change after marriage. That is why divorce rates for men who are too attached to their mothers are generally high."

> - Yuliya Vangorodska,
> www.nydivorcefirm.com
> "How the Mother-Son Relationship Contributes to Divorce"

The responsibility of married couples to each other involves a total commitment. This means literally "forsaking all others." This not only includes in-laws and parents, but also friends, fishing companions, and so on. When a husband and wife marry, they commit themselves to the task of building a good and enriching marriage. We don't usually make lifetime commitments to friends or business associates, but only to our spouses.

> "Joseph and Lois Bird suggest: 'If the relationship with parents, friends, or relatives—their visits, actions, or influence—has a negative effect on our relationship with the one person to whom we have committed ourselves, we can make no rational choice other than to curtail—or even terminate—contacts with our parents (or others). The responsibility rests on each one of us. If necessary we may have to take steps, which could alienate our parents, and they may be deeply hurt.'
>
> "The authors go on to say that this advice isn't intended to hurt anyone, least of all one's parents or friends. It's simply a matter of priorities, and making choices for the marriage, not against anyone."
>
> - Norman Wright
> "The Other Woman in Your Marriage"

Cindy and I realize all too well the damage that an unhealthy family conflict or intrusion can bring into a marriage. It happened to us early in our marriage because I would not defend Cindy to my parents over some interpersonal problems between my wife and another family member.

If you remember from the previous chapter, my mode of dealing with any kind of conflict was to run away. This sinful abdication of responsibility on my part created a lot of tension. Frankly, I was a coward. My "thinking" at the time was: "This is Cindy's and this other person's problem, not mine; they can deal with it themselves."

Sadly, I never tried to help reconcile the differences or defend Cindy's position. Eventually, Cindy recognized how hurt my parents were, and she backed away from the situation, and it brought peace back to the family. It may have brought a "peace" to the family unit, but it did not bring any sort of peace to Cindy (and as a result of my ditching responsibility, nor to me).

Eventually, this family member came to Christ and came to Cindy and confessed to her that they knew they had been the instigator of many problems, and their relationship blossomed. However, there was still that underlying hurt that I caused that still wasn't resolved.

It wasn't until 2004 when Cindy and I were taking some training from Dr. David and Teresa Ferguson for their Intimate Encounters program that I finally realized just how much pain I caused Cindy. This three-day intensive workshop gave Cindy and me a lot of one-on-one time to deal with "hurts from the past." This is when my heart broke (almost literally) as I got behind her eyes for the first time to see what I had done. I wept and asked for her forgiveness. Please note, there is a huge difference between saying, "I'm sorry," and asking for forgiveness. Saying you're sorry when you forget to do something for your wife is good; but when you have caused a deep, lasting pain in her heart, "sorry" won't cut it.

Your spouse will know when you are sincerely brokenhearted and repentant for any breach in the relationship that you're responsible for. Thankfully, Cindy knew I finally "got it," received my repentance, and forgave me.

Let me make this very simple. Any time you do not choose to defend your spouse to another family member over any cause, then you have not "left your family" (according to God's standards for leaving), and you are not fully cleaved (united) to your spouse. And this will always be a source of tension until you cut the cords completely and become a united front as husband and wife.

What About Living with Parents?

Since Cindy talked about this, all I'll add is that a survey taken by Debate.org concerning the question the question they asked: "Should You Live with Your Parents After Marriage?" Only 13 percent of the respondents felt it was a good idea. The other 87 percent felt it would damage the marriage. From everything Cindy and I have seen from people writing to us about their experiences, we don't recommend it if it can possibly be avoided.

Leaving and cleaving can be hard enough for a newlywed couple when you're living on your own. So the difficulty of being able to leave and cleave is amplified a hundredfold as newlyweds if you are living under the same roof with either of your parents.

Potential Destroyers of Marital Unity

We seem to want to pigeonhole leaving and cleaving to only family relationships that can be destructive. But there's a host of other things that can divide us just as much. For instance:

Personal Friendships: We don't care how close you were to the people you grew up with or work with, if their continued friendship makes your spouse uncomfortable, then you may need to sever it. This is especially true if it's a "guy" friend (for the wife) or a "gal" friend (for the husband). We tell people all the time that opposite-sex friendships can be the most destructive thing that can happen in your marriage.

We're not saying you should never hang out with your friends; it's just when those relationships seem to take priority over your marital relationship is when changes need to take place.

Electronic Friendships: Over the past ten years this has become an ever-increasing destructive force in breaking up marriages. Facebook, Instagram, Twitter, Chat Rooms, and just inordinate amounts of time spent surfing the Net is the new way of "cheating" on your spouse. And I'm not talking about just sexual liaisons that develop from hooking up "electronically"; it's anything that can rob you of interpersonal connection with your spouse.

Author and marriage expert Doug Fields warns of the "Digital Invasion." He says,

> "It can sabotage the time you need to spend with your spouse to grow your marriage. Sometimes it's important to turn off your phone and other electronic devices. When you come home from work it's too simple to get lost in texting, checking and reading from the phone [or computer]. Don't make the mistake of believing you're so critical to the world that you must be accessible at all times."

And then, David Boehi warns:

> "We are tempted to think that our little 'sips' of online connection add up to a big gulp of real conversation. But they don't. E-mail, Twitter, Facebook, all of these have their places — in politics, commerce, romance and friendship. But no matter how valuable, they do not substitute for conversation. The drift from conversation to connectivity—from 'talking to texting'— should be a concern for any married couple.
>
> "Other technologies—particularly television—have distracted us from conversation for many years. But recent advances give us the option to replace it. How can you develop and maintain a strong relationship with your spouse if you aren't talking to each other?"
>
> - David Boehi
"Preparing for Marriage: Discover God's Plan for a Lifetime of Love"

One of the more helpful things I found in protecting you is what Pastor Andrew Linder wrote in an Internet article called "5 Easy Ways to Keep Social Media from Ruining Your Marriage."

> "In our marriages, it is vitally important to have some social media and texting rules between spouses. And by doing so, not only will you have a better marriage, you'll avoid a number of potentially devastating dangers that lie in the bottom of Satan's toolbox.
>
> "Here are five rules I'd encourage you and your spouse to get on the same page about:
>
> 1. **Obvious and open accounts.** If you're on social media, there's no room for a lack of clarity when it comes to your marriage. Clearly identify that you're married, and unashamed of it. Allow each other full access to passwords and all accounts. No hidden apps or accounts allowed.
> "Trying to hide the fact that you are married or are in a serious relationship on your social media accounts should be a huge red flag for any couple, just like it would be for you to take off your wedding ring in order to give someone

a false impression that you're available.

2. **No 'casual' encounters with previous or new opposite sex relationships**. Marriage deserves your utmost priority to protect your relationship. This requires that there be clear boundaries. Recently, Vice President Mike Pence came under fire for a rule he holds to in his marriage, that he will not eat alone with anyone of the opposite sex other than his wife. However, that's not absurdity (as some would have us to believe), that's just a wise practice for any married person who chooses to draw some lines of protection in their marriage. "Just like one look at another person can turn into two, and inadvertently snowball to much more, so can an 'innocent' run-in with and old fling via social media. It's happened to so many good people, so don't think you're above becoming a statistic. "Which is worse… potentially hurting the feelings of someone who's not even in your life anymore, or potentially opening a door that could cause untold devastation to the most important relationship in your life? Don't be afraid to draw a line and stick to it.

3. **Avoid confrontation or conflict via text**. Texting is the king of miscommunication. Thankfully we now have emojis to help a little bit with that, but they certainly don't solve this massive problem. If you have to fight, do it in person. If you need to share your feelings, do it in a way that your feelings can be seen, verbally expressed and fully understood. Agree not to fight or argue via text.

4. **No social media or texting with others when you are trying to spend dedicated time together**. If you're on a date with your spouse, then don't be on a date with your phone. If you're having a face-to-face conversation together, don't be trying to carry on a silent text conversation with someone else at the same time. [I'll be the first to admit guilt on this one.] Give your spouse the decency and respect that they deserve—the best of your time, attention and affection.

5. **A mutually understood transparency policy**. I would encourage you to ban secrets from your marriage (emotional, relational, financial and sexual), because transparency is vital in the marriage relationship. God created your spouse to be the one person in life with which you have absolutely nothing to hide. This would rightly include your social media accounts and text history. "The devil is not a rookie at the game of deceit and division. He's had quite a bit of experience, and he knows pretty well what he's doing. The specific tools he uses may change from one generation to the next, but the toolbox itself is still made up of the same three components: the lust of the eyes, the lust of the flesh and the pride of life. Social media is just one more of many tools he can use to accomplish his purpose. "For some, these may simply be good reminders and refreshers. For others, these things may serve as a glaring red flag in your marriage. Either way... don't be naïve. Don't overlook these easy ways to protect your relationship. Don't let the devil stand a chance in your marriage. Your marriage is far too valuable.

"Which of these five rules do you currently practice in your marriage?"

- Andrew Linder
www.ChurchLeaders.com
Used by permission,

We feel Andrew's guidelines nailed it as far as giving all of us the practical ways to protect our unity as a couple in this area of Electronic Friendships.

"As Linder said, 'The devil is no rookie at the game of deceit and division.' That's why we must 'Be alert and of sober mind. Your enemy the devil prowls around like a roaring lion looking for someone to devour.'"

- 1 Peter 5:8
NIV

The best way I can sum up this essential is to share a portion of an excellent article called "Leaving And Cleaving":

> "With this more robust understanding of leaving, it becomes clearer that leaving is a process, not simply an event. The leave, cleave, and weave pattern for marriage outlined in Genesis 2:24 is to continue throughout the course of a relationship. Consequently, a helpful question to frequently ask yourself is: to whom or what am I most loyal today, this month, this past year?
>
> "Whatever your situation and whatever you are still held by, the good news is the more you become aware of and work through these wounds and roles, the more freedom you will experience. And as you experience more freedom, you can more fully align your loyalties to your spouse and improve your ability to love him [or her] as God intended."
>
> - Steve Mesmer
"Today's Christian Woman," July, 2014

Please don't ever minimize these admonitions from the Bible, as it can lead to the demise of your marriage. And remember, "Standing United" is not just a one-time act. Often it is a decision you have to make every day.

MARRIAGE ESSENTIAL #7
PARTNER WITH GOD AND EACH OTHER
TO MAKE AN IMPACT ON YOUR WORLD

In the last essential we brought up the importance of elevating our marriages to model the example given in Ecclesiastes 4:12, NIV:

"Though one may be overpowered, two can defend themselves.
A cord of three strands is not quickly broken."

When we commit to live out this model of partnership with God at the center, it will be a game changer.

Cindy

This is probably my favorite chapter to write. That is because I love being in partnership with my husband Steve. Since the day I learned about marriage partnership and its importance, I have been continually amazed at how much easier, less stressful, happier, and more fulfilling our marriage has become as we have applied this principle to our relationship.

I even remember the incident that introduced this different mindset into our marriage "bent", so to speak. We were having company coming over, and I was running around trying to get everything done before they arrived. Steve came into the room and was ready to sit down and relax for a while. I was incensed when he started to do this. I couldn't believe he would think of relaxing when there was so much that we still needed to accomplish. I snapped at him, "Are you kidding? You invite people over for dinner, and then you expect me to do all of the work myself?"

Steve replied, "I'm tired. And besides, I don't know what to do." Sadly, I said a few very unkind things to him, and then responded, "If you can't see what needs to be done, then I'll give you a list." I was amazed that Steve thought this was a good idea. If given that option, I would have responded, "Why do I need a list? I can see what needs to be done!" But apparently, Steve didn't. Puzzled, I made up a list to get on with what needed to be done. With the list before him, Steve proceeded to do everything that was on it. He especially enjoyed checking off each point after completing that particular task.

I made sure I didn't give him fussy things to do that I wanted done a certain way. I've seen that he is not good at doing little, detailed tasks. I'm talking about things like arranging the table to look nice, rather than in just a practical manner of slapping some plates and tableware on the table. He would just plunk the tableware on the table in whatever way they would fall. I wanted the table to look nicer than that. So, I had him do the bigger things, such as vacuuming, mopping the floor, sweeping the front walkway, etc. Those are chores he can do, and he does them just fine.

As time went on, I saw that we were actually working like a well-oiled machine. Everything got done with time to spare. And we didn't even argue about it. Steve told me the list was helpful. He truly didn't know all that needed to be done. It opened up his mind. And the fact that I made sure the list fit his skill set rather than saying, "just start cleaning," seemed to help him.

Later, after our company left we talked about the whole pre-company incident. Steve confessed that he is often at a loss as to what to do when we're preparing for visitors. I didn't realize that because it just comes naturally to me. And then Steve came up with a great question he can ask when we're in another similar situation. The question is: "What do you want me to do to lighten the workload?" Or it could be, "What can I do to best help you?" Either way, those are great questions. I then promised not to get angry because he doesn't just see what needs to be done as I do. I know this may sound stupid, but it used to anger me that I saw all that needed to be accomplished, but he didn't. I thought he should too. But it is what it is, and it's ridiculous to get angry over "who sees" and "who doesn't see." We need to act like a marital team and "just do it."

We then promised each other that neither of us would sit down to relax until both of us could do so. This was a great step forward in our marriage relationship.

The next time we had company over, that's what happened. Steve asked the question, and I made out a list (which I now do ahead of time). The list is tailored to Steve's "talents." He does some things better or faster than me, and I can do the rest. When we combine all of this together, we get it all done with a whole lot less hassle. We don't fight our talents; we combine them.

We have come to see that I do better on detail work, and being a household manager. Steve does better on being the yard and vehicle manager, and we overlap in other areas. It works great for us. Another couple may need to flip some things around, and that's okay. The point is that we approach issues as a team to get the job done. We both invest in the partnership aspect of our marriage.

I now sit back and wonder, Why did I fight this for so long? Why did I expend so much energy at trying to change Steve, thinking he should just "know" these things like I did? (Although, there are other things that he just "knows" that I don't... but I never saw it that way.) Why didn't I/we instead look for ways to work together in partnership? I really don't know. But I do it now—we both do. I/we can still fall into that trap sometimes. But we're both on the positive side of leaning into learning how to apply our gifts and talents to work together. It is a "we" thing, rather than a "his" as opposed to "mine." It's a whole different mindset and focus. I highly suggest you do this as a married couple too. Try it; you may like it! Or you will at least find that it curbs so many of the misunderstandings that can be ushered into these types of situations.

Being Oppositional

What's strange is the fact that I wasn't even aware that I was being oppositional to Steve (and he was to me). We just sort of fell into this type of approach to matters as they popped up in our lives. We approached housework, yard work, money matters, raising children, taking care of our health, worship styles, even how we prayed and studied the Bible (and the list goes on) from differing and opposing stances. And the arguments? They were ridiculous, as I look back on them. So many of them could have been avoided, or shortened, or dealt with in healthier ways if we would have approached them as partners, not opponents.

Fellow author and blogger Fawn Weaver (from The Happy Wife's Club website) said:

> "The greatest marriages are built on teamwork. A mutual respect, a healthy dose of admiration, and a never-ending portion of love and grace."

Well, we didn't give each other very much grace in the beginning of our marriage. We started out with lots of admiration and what we thought was love. But it eventually fizzled and was thrown aside by our ever-increasing "selfism" and busyness that came along with trying to make life work for us. Through our website, we've seen that a lot of marriages end up in this same place.

Busyness and Partnership

It has been said that when you are too busy to be kind, you are too busy. I mentioned this before in another marriage essential, but I want to revisit it a bit more. We definitely allowed ourselves to get caught up in the busier side of life. And as a result, kindness became more of a distant memory than something we gave to each other. We allowed life to squeeze into the middle of our relationship and push us onto opposing sides.

Yes, life can get busy, especially when you're raising children. We are involved with jobs, careers, family, friends, maintaining a home, and such. But Steve and I made choices to allow too much busyness into our lives. We now recognize that was problematic, but at the time we thought that it was just the way life was supposed to be. Wrong!

Through this marriage journey down the wrong path, I've learned that just because you can do something, it doesn't mean that you should do it. I needed (and Steve needed) to say no to more things, so we could say yes to invest the time and energy into our marriage and family life. We gave each other only leftover time and energy instead of saving some of it to spend more time with each other. A steady diet of leftovers can cause undernourishment in a marriage relationship. We also sometimes need that, which is prime, to feed our companionship needs.

Marrying Our Lives

We needed the advice that Jared Black gave:

> "Marriage isn't something we accomplished the day we said 'I do.' It is an ongoing action discovered with our spouses—a development cycle. The day of marriage simply creates a brand-new infant couple, pledging to learn the art of marrying their individual lives into one combined, maturing life together."
>
> - Tyler Ward's book
> "Marriage Rebranded," p. 74

Steve and I didn't realize in the "infancy stage" of marrying that we were marrying more than our bodies together. We didn't even know that it was an infancy stage. We thought we had arrived at the destination of our dreams. But we now know that it is just a beginning. It's much like the kindergarten stage of education. From our wedding day forward, we are given the task of marrying our "individual lives into one combined, maturing life together." That's a huge mission.

It's especially huge when you realize this means that we have to lean towards maturity. Selfism is to be left behind. Marriage has no room for that. As I've said before, marriage is for grown-ups, not for those who want to cling onto just satisfying themselves. If you want to continue to act like children, you shouldn't get married. I often refer the following scripture when talking about marriages. The Apostle Paul said:

> "When I was a child I talked like a child; I thought like a child; I reasoned like a child. When I became a man [grew up] I put childish ways behind me."
>
> - 1 Corinthians 13:11
> NIV

What I see in that verse is that "there is a time for everything under Heaven." There is a time to act like a child. But there is a time to grow up and put childish things behind us. Marriage is one of those times. For a marriage to be healthy, growing, and one that blesses us, and others—especially God—we must live within it through mature eyes, with mature attitudes, and actions. If we don't, we can ruin a whole lot of other people's lives, as well as our own, as we're playing around.

Marriage is a vehicle God uses to help to grow us up, to mature us in ways that He wants so He can use us for His Kingdom work. That's important to recognize. It's like what H. Norman Wright says:

> "Marriage is more than sharing a life together. It's building a life together. What you do now is for both, and what is said now is for both. What your purpose is now is for the kingdom and giving glory to the image of God."
>
> - Norm Wright
> "One Marriage Under God," p. 44

Thinking in the Same Direction

It's not that once we marry, we are to be joined at the hip as we are building this life together. But we are to grow to be so "like-minded" that we keep each other in consideration with everything we do. It's that whole concept described in the Bible of how the body parts work together separately, and yet together, they make up one body that is whole. We may not always think alike, but we can work to think together, finding ways to compromise so we are both satisfied with the results.

In a preceding marriage essential, I mentioned that I love marriage, and how much I love my marriage. As I said, I can't even start to imagine what my life would be like had I not married Steve. I want that type of happiness, challenge, and companionship for everyone possible. Our life is so good together. And that's the operative word here, "together."

Steve and I are two independent people, who are very different from each other. But now that we are married, our life is to be approached more from a "we" posture, rather than just a "me" posture. We have learned, and are learning to do this. We recognize that we have vowed not to do anything that would hurt the "we" in our marriage. A "cleaved" couple does not hurt their partner.

Yes, we do have some hobbies, activities, and friendships that we are active in apart from each other. Being married does not erase the other from having some independence in different ways. It actually makes our relationship more interesting as we talk about our individual pursuits and experiences. It also gives us the opportunity to pray for and cheer each other on, concerning those activities. This further joins us together. But the point is that even marriage partners need some breathing space. I agree with what Marie Reed Crowell said:

> "To keep the fire burning brightly there's one easy rule: Keep the two logs together, near enough to keep each other warm and far enough apart—about a finger's breadth—for breathing room. Good fire, good marriage, same rule."

Apart and Together

Having some interests that are separate can be healthy for our marriages, as long as we also have mutual interests we pursue together. But it's especially important that our separate interests are not lived out at the expense of the other. In other words, if there is something Steve or I want to do, we won't do it if it will hurt our partner. That is all part of living out our vow to "love, honor, and cherish" each other. I'm not doing much cherishing if I decide I want to do something or be with someone that will hurt Steve.

Sometimes, it's a matter of timing that needs to be talked about and agreed upon. It's like something I heard (which is true): "Constant connections with the outside world can leave us disconnected from our marriage partner." It's important to learn the art of connecting and disconnecting. There is a "time for everything under Heaven" as we're told in the Bible.

Disturbances in Partnership

Sometimes, there are disturbances in partnership from the inside, and other times from the outside. We've seen some spouses who have very expensive hobbies or interests, and it is a true burden on their marital budget. If the other spouse is okay with that, and it works for them financially, then that's fine. But if he or she isn't, then there's a problem. It causes a disturbance in the partnership, from within their circle of two. You have to deal with it and come to a mutual place of satisfaction.

Norm Wright, in his book "One Marriage Under God" (p. 47) tells of a family incident that happened to Dale and his (now deceased) wife, Sherry. Dale told Norm:

> "I was so used to being single, and even being a 'married single' in my first marriage, that I didn't give much regard to someone else when I made decisions. I was on my own. But soon after Sherry and I married, I 'just' invited my parents and my brother and his wife over for dinner. I told Sherry they were coming over Friday night, and after a few seconds she said, 'Dale, I love your family and certainly want them over, but that won't cut it. We need to talk it over with one another first before we make a decision. I won't refuse you. I just want to be included.' I needed to learn that it was now 'we' and not 'me.' My old habits needed to change. And I'm glad I had a wife who would help me make this change. 'We' is so much better than 'me'!"

When we're single, we can go about life with only the concerns of us and God. But when there is a spouse involved (and possibly kids), we no longer have the same freedom. (See: 1 Corinthians 7.) On the other hand, we have other benefits of companionship; i.e., God's blessing on our sexual life together, and more. But we dare not act as if we are single if we are married, nor act married if we are still single. Too many people get this all mixed up in their thinking and actions.

Changes and Choices to Partner Together

Here's another important point I want to make. Whether you are single or married, the important thing to learn is how to go with the flow of the changes that come into your life. Concerning marriage partnership, I'm reminded of something Norm Wright said in his book, "One Marriage Under God" (p. 153) regarding difficulties that come our way:

> "As changes occur in your lives, it is your challenge as a married couple to use them to draw yourselves closer together rather than allow them to tear you apart. Throughout your married life you will suffer losses—some small, some large, some even devastating. You may have to endure miscarriages, stillbirths, job or career losses, illnesses, accidents, and any other of literally hundreds of setbacks. How you respond to each will affect your marriage relationship. It will also affect the story your marriage tells."

The enemy of our faith works hard to push us apart from helping one another as marriage partners. The goal is to isolate us so we experience aloneness and despair. Dennis Rainey makes a great point on this issue:

> "Isolation is a subtle killer of relationships. Genesis 2:24 gives us a prescription from Scripture: Leave, cleave, and become one. The enemy of our souls does not want a husband and wife to be one. Instead, he wants to divide us. In John 17, Jesus prayed for the church to be one. He realized that when we're in isolation, we could be convinced of anything. Isolation kills relationships."

- Familylife.com
Article, "40 Lessons From 40 Years of Marriage"

When different challenges and troubles interrupt our life together, we need to put forth intentionality in not allowing it to divide us.

Agree to Partner

Make the agreement: "We will do whatever is needed to stabilize this marriage." If something tragic happens, you may need to give each other grace and space to grieve in your own ways. But whatever you do, don't judge your spouse for the way he or she is grieving. It probably won't be your way of handling grief, but don't be his or her judge on this matter. Be as supportive as you can be.

And if you notice emotional distance between you growing in an unhealthy way, then give each other the permission to say something. Just make sure you don't press in on your spouse to the degree that your spouse feels stifled.

Author Karilee Hayden gives the following excellent advice. She recommends "cocooning" (which is something I referred to in another marriage essential). Here's a portion of what she says:

> "Crisis takes our breath away, sometimes completely knocking us off our feet. An unexpected death. Sudden illness. Natural catastrophe or family emergency. A good name ruined. Financial disaster. Critical times stir up anguish, fear or anger so fierce it can destroy a marriage. If we turn inward, withdrawing from our spouse, we risk damaging the beautiful oneness of marriage.
>
> "So how do couples respond to crisis? What helps? I believe God wants us to cocoon together, as husband and wife. Doing so strengthens a relationship, eases heartache and deepens love for each other through the shared pain."

Thrivingpastor.com
Article, "Cocooning in Crisis"

Karen gives excellent advice in this article concerning times of crisis and how to cocoon. She says to "run to God," and also "pare down" to get rid of excess activity. Additionally, "insulate; don't isolate" and "plan respites." You can read her article to learn more.

Again, what you are trying to do is first stabilize the marriage so more damage isn't being done, and then work on doing things in the future in healthy, rather than destructive ways. We have an article titled "A Marriage in Crisis—Doing What It Takes to Save It" (posted in the "Save My Marriage" topic) that gives additional suggestions.

It's important to note:

> "No relationship is all sunshine. But once you've learned how to play in the rain, you've discovered the secret to surviving passing storms together."
>
> - Fawn Weaver

This is something you need to learn so you can do it. It doesn't come naturally. It's all part of our wedding vows to love "for better or worse, in sickness or in health, till death parts us."

> "Marriage is meant to keep people together, not just when things are good, but particularly when they are not. That's why we take marriage vows, not wishes."
>
> - Ngina Otiende

Health Issues Can Divide Us

When we're talking about marriage partnership, we're faced with the inevitable. In most every marriage, there will be health issues that will arise. Some of them will be less serious than others. But they will happen. The issue, though, is do we allow them to cause division, or do we help each other through them?

Earlier in our marriage, Steve and I truly acted immature a lot of the time when one of us got sick. We often got upset with each other because of the inconvenience of it all. When one of us would have the flu or another illness, the other had to step up and take on more responsibilities. That's all a part of marriage. Sometimes, the workload rests more on one than it does the other. Marriage is not a 50/50 agreement. It's supposed to be a 100/100 agreement where both partners give 100 percent in the effort they put forth.

If one is down, though, the other is there to help to lift that spouse up. As we're told in Ecclesiastes 4:9-10, NIV, "Two are better than one, because they have a good reward for their work: If one falls down, his friend can help him up. But pity the man who falls and has no one to help him up!" This can involve lifting and helping our marriage partner up emotionally, mentally, physically, spiritually, and/or financially.

Steve and I have had to do some light lifting and sometimes heavy lifting at different times in our marriage. We've learned and are learning to do better now in this lifting matter. To have a good marriage, you just have to learn how to go with the flow of challenges when they attack one or both of you.

Health Issue Crisis

One of our challenges in our marriage has come through the vehicle of Type-1 Diabetes. As we shared previously, Steve came down with it when we were about two years into our marriage. To say that it has brought its share of challenges our way is an understatement. Unless you live with diabetes or you live with a spouse who is a diabetic, you really can't understand how horrible this disease can become and how it can challenge you in ways you never thought possible.

Type-1 Diabetes is difficult for my husband, Steve, and it is difficult for me as his partner. It can truly be trying on the strength our marital commitment, at times.

With Steve, it can bring in dementia episodes where he doesn't know who he is, who I am, where he is, or anything. He becomes completely irrational and can lose control in almost every way.

There have been times when I've wondered how I could continue on in our future. All of this is frightening, confusing, and difficult, to say the least.

I remember one particular episode, when I wanted to throw in the towel on our marriage. I was overwhelmed with fear and confusion. And I couldn't imagine making it through another episode.

We were in Nashville at a National Religious Broadcasters Convention. While we were with a group of Christian broadcasting colleagues at a concert, I noticed Steve was starting to go into an insulin reaction; his sugar levels were going down. When it happens it's like he is drunk. He acts like a completely different person and can be incoherent, etc. Plus, he can also slip into a coma if it isn't tended to right away.

I excused us from our colleagues (figuring it was important that they didn't see what was happening to Steve; I was afraid it would jeopardize his job). I then managed to get Steve out of the building to get him away from the crowd. I knew that it would just complicate matters to stay in that crowd. Also, I didn't know how fast his sugar levels would go down. At that time in his life, it would plummet pretty fast. I knew that I had to get him to a location where I could get his attention (without distraction) and get some sugar into him so his levels would go up again.

Unfortunately, all I had were a few little sugar candies in my purse. I knew I needed to get him to a place where I could get juice into him to raise his sugar levels. I got him to start sucking on the candies and tried to walk him back to our hotel to get the juice. Sadly, I couldn't remember the way back to the hotel. I was turned around. So, I was trying to get directions to go back, and I was trying to manage Steve so he didn't run into the street. His sugar levels were so low that I didn't know what he would do. It was becoming more and more dangerous every minute that passed.

Through a long turn of events, somehow, I got us back to the hotel, holding on to Steve, who was weaving around, acting irrationally at that point. The elevator ride up to our room was embarrassing and extremely upsetting, as others were riding up with us. I'm sure they thought he was drunk. For some reason, I didn't even think to tell them what was going on so we could perhaps get help from these strangers. All I knew was that I had to somehow get Steve to our room. At one turn down the hall, Steve started to run away from me. He had lost memory of who I was and where we were. He was afraid of the stranger (me) who appeared to be dragging him to some unknown location.

I've never prayed so hard in all my life. I knew that he could start screaming, hurt himself, or hurt someone else in his haste to flee. With all my heart, I believe God helped me to get to the hotel, get Steve into the elevator, and then convince him to come with me into our room (that he no longer recognized).

Once in our room, I managed to convince Steve to sit down and start drinking the juice I had there for him. Eventually, the juice started to do what was needed. Steve's sugar levels started to balance. When they did, he looked up at me and said, "What just happened? Why are we here?"

To explain the flood of emotions that I felt at that point would take volumes of paragraphs to explain. What I'm writing here is just a thumbnail sketch of all that happened from the moment I sensed Steve was going into an insulin reaction to the point of his regaining his senses. I remember just looking at Steve and telling him that I needed him to just sit quietly, drink his juice, and leave me alone for a while. I started to unravel emotionally and needed to talk to God big time at that point.

Talking to God Through the Confusion

I ran a bubble bath, closed the door of the bathroom (I knew Steve would be okay at that point), and sat in the bathtub crying deeply. I poured out my emotions to God—concerning the fear, the confusion, the emotional and physical drain I experienced, and the feeling that this was totally unfair to put me through this. I had a major pity party breakdown, held right there in the bathroom.

I told God that I was done. I didn't want to ever have to do anything like this again. I was tired, scared, and couldn't imagine ever having the strength to repeat what I had just done. I wanted out of our marriage. I didn't marry a diabetic. As I said earlier, I swore earlier in my life that I would never marry a diabetic. But here I was married to one. Steve came down with it after we had married. I told God this was not part of the deal I signed up for in marrying Steve. I wanted to divorce him and live a "normal" life (whatever that is), just like my other friends.

God waited until after I had ranted, raved, cried, and totally let Him have it for letting this happen, before He said anything to me. (My pity parties are not pretty, nor do they lack in going in ugly directions.) When I was all done, God spoke to my heart in a still, small voice. He said within my thoughts, "Yes this is part of the 'deal' you signed up for when marrying. Do you remember the 'for better or for worse, in sickness and in health, till parted by death' vows that you made to me and to Steve? Well, this is part of the worst. You didn't think it would get this bad, but sometimes it does. And what about Steve? Do you think he wants to go through this? Do you think he wants to have diabetes? Should you just throw him out because he comes down with this disease?"

God said a lot of other things to me, but through it all, I got the point. God cared, but God also had a plan. And my staying in the marriage and being Steve's marriage partner for life is all a part of His plan. I cleaned myself up—physically, emotionally, and spiritually—then left the bathroom and fell into Steve's arms. We talked, cried, and pledged our love and commitment to each other.

And from that day on, we're still plodding along on this. We've had many more difficult situations smack us in the face. One of these included Steve going through the "widow-maker" heart attack. What a trip that has been! But it has been a blessing and has brought blessings to others in ministry opportunities, as we look back on it. God has been merciful and has helped us through that. Steve is very much alive, and we are very much thankful and appreciative of God's mercy.

I say all of this to make a point. It is to bring out the fact that marriage partnership takes us down some scary and "unfair" and confusing roads sometimes. But as we lean into God, we can learn some important, life-changing things, and God can use them in His Kingdom work.

I so agree with what Joni Tada writes about suffering and trials, and what we can learn from them. She says when we come upon trials:

> "We do everything we can to escape it: we medicate it, mask it, surgically remove it, entertain or drug it, institutionalize it, divorce it, or even euthanize it—anything but live with it. Suffering, however, isn't about to go away. And marriage only magnifies it."

How very true. And so is the following that Joni also says:

> "It's trials that really press you into the breast of your Savior. It's the cord of three strands. Realize that your enemy is not your spouse or even the disability or the bankruptcy or the disagreement or whatever it is that is troubling you. The enemy is Satan himself. He hates marriage, and he has hated it since the very first union in a fragrant, misty garden called Eden. This fierce adversary will do everything in his power to suffocate married love. So be alert! Keep casting yourself on Jesus Christ, steadily relying on Him, even when you don't like it."

- Joni & Ken
"An Untold Love Story"

This is when our partnership with God and with each other is especially threatened. It is then that we most need to "be on the alert" as we're told in the Bible. Isolating us and dividing us is the main mission of the enemy of our faith. It is known that marriage is portrayed as a living picture of the love of Christ for His bride, the church. So why wouldn't the enemy want to tear apart that picture? Our mission is to make sure we don't participate in that destruction.

Love God and Each Other

Steve and I do a lot of marriage mentoring. We do this personally and through the ministry of Marriage Missions. Recently, there was a husband who met with Steve concerning his marriage. It is a mess! Here are two people who love the Lord, and yet they can't seem to find the pathway to treating each other with love. Their relationship is volatile and toxic. And what makes it even worse is that they have teenagers who are watching this destructive behavior. With one side of their mouth they claim to love the Lord and tell these teenagers about the love of God, and with the other side they yell, scream, and act out with each other in horrible ways.

It's so difficult to see this going on in their relationship and their house. I call it a "house" and not a home because people don't live like that in a home—just a shell of a house. A home is one where love is seen and heard. This couple has so much potential to "live a life of love" as we're told to do in Ephesians 5:2. But they get stuck in their own stuff and give themselves the permission to do that, which they know they shouldn't. How tragically sad!

When our sons were younger and still living at home, we used to have a rule in our home (and still do) that "Home base is safe." As we told our sons, "The world out there is crazy; but in our home, we're safe with each other." We didn't (and still don't) allow in our home any type of name-calling or devaluing each other with words or with actions. We've made it a point that everyone who enters our home is safe from ridicule. Our home is a haven the Lord has given us for everyone's protection.

So let me ask you: is your marriage a safe place for your spouse? When they hurt in some way, do you treat them in a loving manner so that they don't need to look elsewhere to find comfort? (The exception is when it's a counseling type of interaction.) Do they know that you're waiting with open arms, an open mind and heart to listen to, and comfort them when they need it? And do they know that you won't make them the object of being further humiliated?

Some spouses will look for comfort and pleasure in all the wrong places. You may not be able to change that. Prayerfully you can. But even if you can't, you don't want to give them any excuse or push them further into temptation by your hurtful words and/or actions. That much you can do. It's important not to be a "stumbling block" that contributes to helping our spouse fall all the further.

In marriage, we're supposed to act like partners together to fight against any storm that comes our way. Let's face it; if we use our strength in fighting with each other, then how much energy do we have left to fight against the various types of storms that will also come upon us?

Even if you have a spouse who doesn't cooperate in easing the tension, it's still important not to contribute to the frustration level that's happening within your marriage. That doesn't mean that you can't voice your opinion when things are not going in a good direction. But do you "speak the truth in love" with a sincerely caring spirit, or do you step over a line where you are contentious?

It's amazing the amount of times we hear the statement, "I know I'm not perfect—I have my faults too, but my spouse . . ." and out comes a list of his or her faults. For some reason, we think our faults are excusable (just as our spouse thinks his or hers are excusable), and yet we don't give him/her the same grace that we want given to us. His or her faults are inexcusable, but ours are excusable and can be rationalized. Many of us need to rethink this.

Again, we are to live like partners, speak as partners, and face every obstacle as partners. We are to be partners with God and with each other. We didn't vow to each other to live a life of being adversaries, nor to live like we are enemies.

Sadly, there have been times in our marriage when we have been at an "enemy" stage. We treated each other more like adversaries than marital partners. But thank God, He has helped us to open our eyes and, instead, work on being best friends.

Juli Slattery wrote something that I believe is noteworthy to remember:

> "Picture where you and your husband might be in a few decades, in the winter of your marriage. Your kids will be grown and gone... How will you fill an empty house and hours of silence? Through friendship, the powerful bond that will keep you connected through each season of joy and grief. It's worth working toward now!"
>
> - Authenticintimacy.com
> Article, "My Husband Isn't My Best Friend"

I remember a number of years ago when our youngest son was planning on moving out of the house to be closer to the college he was attending. It was a bit premature, and eventually, he decided to wait until he finished school (which we agreed with).

But his older brother called and asked me how I was doing with the thought of having an "empty nest" after having lived so many years of busyness with our "kids" livening up our home. I laughed and told him that while I loved being a mom and having them around so much... his dad and I would do "just fine" being "alone together." We loved being with them, but we didn't need to be with them all the time... we would be "just fine—not to worry!"

And we have been. We really miss our sons and their families because they geographically live so far away from us. But my husband is truly my best friend—my marriage partner that I hope to spend many more years partnering with, "until death parts us."

We have a pillow on our rocking chair that sums up how Steve and I feel about each other. "Happiness is being married to your very best friend." That is true for us, and we pray that it is or will be true for you, as you follow some very good advice from the Bible in Ephesians 5:1-2, ESV:

> "Therefore, be imitators of God, as beloved children. And walk in love, as Christ loved us and gave himself up for us, a fragrant offering and sacrifice to God."

Do you want to know what the "therefore" in those scriptures is there for? Go to the Bible. Read what God tells us to do. The principles for living together in love as a husband and wife are also the principles for loving that the Bible tells us. The Bible is our Principle Guide Book for how we are to treat each other. This especially applies to how we live with the spouse.

May we never forget this, and may we always apply that which God would have us, so we "live a life of love" in our marriage for the rest of our lives here on this earth!

> "May the Lord direct your heart into God's love and Christ's perseverance."
>
> - 2 Thessalonians 3:5
> NIV

STEVE

> "For the first thirty years, my life was about me. It wasn't about anyone else. And now that I'm married, I realize 'my life is not about me; it's about us.' If I'm serious about making my marriage work, then I've got to make that commitment. Sure, there's personal development and I still need personal time. But there's also that relationship, and if it's important to me, I must put the time and effort into it—even if I don't feel like it, even when I'm tired or cranky or ornery."
>
> - Stephen R. Covey,
> "7 Habits of Highly Effective Families," p. 183

That's what Cindy and I believe—marriage is no longer about "me;" it's all about us in partnership. So, as Cindy and I conclude our thoughts on "The 7 Essentials to GROW YOUR MARRIAGE," we wanted to touch on what it really means to be in partnership. To help me hone in on my points, I want to share with you a definition I found at BusinessDictionary.com. A partner is an "individual who joins with other individuals (partners) in an arrangement (partnership) where gains and losses, risks and rewards, are shared among the partners."

To me the phrase, "where gains and losses, risks and rewards, are shared among the partners" sounds a lot like the wedding vows Cindy and I took. You know the part... "for better, for worse, for richer, for poorer, in sickness and in health . . ." As I mentioned earlier, we were just barely in our second year of marriage when the worse—the sickness and the poorer—seemed to slam into us head-on (i.e., the losses and risks of partnership).

Like probably ninety-nine percent of newlyweds we weren't prepared. Our marriage partnership was strained to the max. But we've gone from near divorce to a thriving, happy partnership for forty-three of our forty-six years together. Using the very words from our marriage vows to illuminate this, here is what the progression of our partnership has looked like over the years:

In Sickness

In April of 1974, I went from being a healthy twenty-three-year-old to a Type-1 (juvenile onset) diabetic overnight. I calculated recently that since my diagnosis I have given myself over 79,000 injections of insulin (roughly five shots per day—minimum) to keep me alive. And because I had a heart attack, losing thirty-five percent of my heart function in 2016, I now take meds to reduce risks for another cardiac incident.

For Poorer

I don't want to paint a picture that we were destitute because of my health problems because God blessed us with good health insurance most of the thirty-five years I was working. However, because a lot of the meds I'm required to take to stay alive don't have generic versions, my co-pays have been very high. So, there have been financial strains we've had to endure throughout our marriage.

The other thing that impacted our finances was I worked for a nonprofit ministry for thirty-eight years. We learned to do without some things we "wanted" in order to have the things we "needed." But ministry, as God calls us, has always been more important to us than having financial success. For a number of years—like many of you—we lived paycheck to paycheck.

For Worse

I was responsible for putting a huge strain on our marriage partnership. This was primarily due to the fact that my diabetes went uncontrolled for many years. This was because I did not take responsibility for managing my disease.

I defaulted to Cindy to "try" to manage it.

This was completely unfair to her, and to this day I am ashamed of my behavior and have repented of it to Cindy, who graciously granted me her unconditional forgiveness.

For most of our married life, Cindy never got a good night's sleep because she had to be hypervigilant of the possibility that my blood sugar would drop to a dangerously low level in the middle of the night when I would be unaware. Sometimes, this would happen numerous times per week. Plus, there were many, many times my blood sugar would drop dangerously low during the day, and I would be unaware until I would almost pass out.

Cindy mentioned in her part of this essential about the dementia episodes that I would sometimes experience because of the sudden drops in blood sugar levels. These were very scary times for her. And even now as I recount this, I have tears in my eyes because of the pain and fear I caused Cindy during those times.

The fact is that Cindy not only stood beside me during these awful experiences, she was also my strongest supporter, and this is a testament to our strong partnership. There was one time we went to my diabetes specialist together because of the increasing number of these hypoglycemic episodes. The doctor looked at Cindy and told her she would most likely become a young widow (basically, he threw up his hands and said there was nothing more he could do for me). As we were walking to the car afterward, she looked at me and said, "Did you hear what I heard? I will not accept that! We are going to find a new doctor who can help you."

It was after that experience that God convicted me that I needed to take responsibility to manage my disease and not let it manage me. I did research and sought out the best doctors, which led us to the Diabetes Clinic at the University of Michigan Hospital. There they assured both of us that they could help me.

In Health

I won't go into a lot of detail, but the transformation in my health relating to my diabetes was dramatic (almost miraculous). So much so that when we had to move from Michigan and leave the care of this clinic, my doctor told me that I had "beaten the odds." That's because I had gone more than twenty years without having any peripheral complications most diabetic's experience. I never had any neuropathy, retinopathy, kidney, or liver issues, or foot problems. Because of that, he said, I probably never will. Of course, Cindy and I were quick to give credit to the "Great Physician" for this.

To this day (forty-four years into being a diabetic) I continue to baffle my doctors with the control I have and that I have had no complications closely aligned with being a diabetic. This has given Cindy and me our lives back.

Why did I share this story? Primarily because Cindy and I know that one of the greatest problems that can affect a good partnership is when one spouse (and I'll be bold enough to say it's usually the husband) has a chronic illness and refuses to take responsibility for managing it.

If this resonates with you, this is your wake-up call. It's time to make the changes to relieve your spouse from having to be the one who tries to manage your disease for you and has to watch you kill yourself slowly. God will help you just as He helped me when I understood my responsibility. By doing this you will give your spouse one of the biggest "Love Gifts" possible.

In some circumstances, the other spouse has to take on more of a caretaker role than either of you would want. That is a different circumstance than I am referring to here. When it needs to be, it should be. But to the best of your ability, try to be a partner who doesn't lean upon the other more than it is necessary.

For Better

If you want your marriage to live in the land of "For Better," here are some things you can do to strengthen your partnership and grow your marriage. These are all things Cindy and I have done and seen positive results. I call these: "You know you're in partnership when:

...You Comfort Each Other When You're Down.

The Bible says:

> "Blessed be the God and Father of our Lord Jesus Christ, the Father of mercies and God of all comfort, who comforts us in all our affliction, so that we may be able to comfort those who are in any affliction, with the comfort with which we ourselves are comforted by God."
>
> - 2 Corinthians 1:3-4
> ESV

Cindy and I have tried to practice being the conduit that God uses to bring comfort to each other when we go through those "down times" (physically, emotionally, and spiritually). We all have them, so we all need to learn how to be comfort givers.

You Encourage Each Other to Pursue Your Dreams

Cindy has always been my biggest cheerleader and I have been hers. We both know God has planted in us desires and passions to serve Him in different ways.

I could never have become the chaplain in the fire department I serve in now if Cindy hadn't encouraged me every step of the way. And she could have never taken the lead in birthing Marriage Missions International if I hadn't supported her dream. (We now very much partner in this ministry together.) When you support and encourage each other's dreams, you may never know the impact that will have on the world.

You Still Flirt with Each Other

My heart still skips a beat when Cindy walks into the room. This doesn't happen by chance. It's because we have continued through our forty-six-plus years of marriage to intentionally flirt with each other. I'll (not so innocently) brush up against her when I walk by or gently touch her; and she'll do the same to me. If we're sitting across the room from each other when we're with other people, I'll catch her attention and wiggle my eyebrows up and down real fast. She will in turn bat her eyelashes back at me. Most people never notice, but we both get the silent message loud and clear: "I love you!" And our hearts are warmed.

Our twelve- and eight-year-old grandkids were with us for two months and they caught us doing this. They asked why we did this so much. We told them it was our silent way of flirting with each other and saying, "I love you," silently. They just looked at us and smiled. We knew it built security in them and was an example of what love "looked like."

You Say, "I Love You" Often

One of the first things we say to each other when we wake up and the last thing we say to each other in bed before we go to sleep are these three words. We'll also say them several times throughout the day. If one of us leaves the house, even on a short errand, or at the end of every phone call, we say, "I love you." Even during those times can be termed as being under the "worse" category above, we still say those three words.

They are three easy words, but they go unsaid too often in many marriages.

Don't be afraid to voice your feelings.

If you employ just these five things in your marriage you'll reap unimaginable benefits when it comes to building an unbreakable partnership. Now, you can say, "Well, that's just your opinion. Do any 'nonreligious' experts back up these claims?" Well, I'm glad you asked.

I came across a book called "Beyond the Myth of Marital Happiness," written by Blaine J. Fowers, Ph.D.

In it was a chapter on marital partnership where Dr. Fowers said, "When partners in a marriage value equality, they see each other as equals, treat each other with respect, consider each other's needs, and support one another." In it he talks about the:

Benefits of Equal Partnership

"An equal partnership benefits marriages as a whole and benefits husbands and wives individually.

"**Happier marriages**. Equal partnership fosters closeness between husband and wife, resulting in a stronger and happier marriage. Spouses feel better about themselves and each other, which makes them more likely to share their thoughts and feelings.

"**Benefits to men**. Men benefit emotionally from equal partnership because there is greater openness and they feel better about their marriage. They also benefit from the greater physical intimacy that comes with equal partnership.

"**Benefits to women**. The closer communication and emotional intimacy in an equal partnership greatly benefit women. Research shows that having an equal say in decision-making is the most important contributor to wives' perception of their marriages as happy and satisfying."

Then Fowers goes on to say:

"**Share more routine household tasks**. There are two different kinds of housework, 'occasional' and 'routine.' Occasional jobs, like household repairs, yard work, and paying bills, don't have to be done every day and can be done just about anytime. Routine housework, on the other hand, like cooking, cleaning, doing laundry, and washing dishes is more time-consuming and must be done regularly and repeatedly. Most people, male or female, find these routine jobs dull and tedious. In general, women do more than their share of routine housework. When men are willing to pick up more of these routine tasks rather than relegating most of them to women, they help create a more equal partnership.

"**Work as a team**. Wives who are dissatisfied with the division of labor in the home often say they feel lonely and lack companionship. When wives and husbands work together as a team, without hierarchy or a 'me helping you do your work' attitude, marital happiness increases. Do dishes together. Attack the front room together with one person dusting while the other vacuums. Wash the car together and throw in a sudsy water fight. Set aside time once a month to do a special job as a family, such as planting a garden, cleaning out the garage, or washing windows. Working as a team makes the job go faster, and it's more fun.

"**Avoid 'gate-keeping.'** Researchers have coined the term 'gate-keeping' for behavior that prevents men and women from working as team on household tasks and child-care. For example, some husbands insist that only they know how to mow and trim the lawn properly, closing the gate on wives or children who might enjoy that chore.

"For women, gate-keeping can be especially complex because management of the home is so central to their identity. A woman, who believes housekeeping is primarily 'women's work,' for example, might be hesitant to share that role. She bases her identity largely on how she thinks others view her housekeeping and mothering, so if her husband tries to contribute she might feel a threat to her self-respect and identity.

"A woman with these beliefs who then shares the housekeeping role equally with her husband may feel she is neglecting her family role and may experience guilt, regret and ambivalence. She might not voice her feelings but instead will close the gate in subtle ways, such as holding to rigid housekeeping standards.

"If her husband tries to do his share of household chores, she may redo what he's done or criticize and demean his efforts. He then gives up, giving her back her exclusive domain. To reduce gatekeeping, meet together as a couple (include children where appropriate), make a detailed list of all the household chores, and decide on an arrangement for sharing housework that works for everyone. Make assignments, demonstrate and train as necessary, and set up a time to review how things are going. Have reasonable standards and give every family member the freedom to live up to those standards in his or her own way.

"**Talk about how you divide up housework**. Take the time to talk about how chores are divided up and how each feels about the equality of the division. Express appreciation, listen sympathetically, and make decisions together. These actions will build a sense of fairness in your marriage, which in turn will make your marriage stronger and happier. Typically wives are much more personally invested in care of home and family.

"They also are more affected if the arrangement is not equal. Research suggests men are relatively unaffected by the division of household labor. Thus it's usually up to wives to initiate discussion about rearrangement of housework if they feel it's unfairly divided. A husband committed to an equal partnership will look for signals of increased stress in his wife that could be a result of her taking on more than her share of home and family management.

"**Express appreciation**. Everyone needs to feel appreciated for the things they do. Family scholars note that when couples argue about domestic work, it is seldom over who does what. More often it is over feeling unappreciated for one's efforts. Most spouses disagree about who does what and how much. Typically wives think they do more than their husbands say they do, and husbands think they do more than their wives give them credit for. To help ease these differences, express appreciation for what your spouse does do.

"**Avoid making important decisions independently**. Marriages are happier for both husbands and wives when each has an equal say in important decisions, such as where the family lives, how to rear the children, and how money is spent. Don't make these important decisions without fully discussing them with your spouse. In the financial area, some couples set an amount of money above which they won't spend without first consulting the other.

"**Share child-care responsibilities**. Children benefit when both fathers and mothers are actively involved in their lives. Research shows that mothers and fathers have independent effects on their children, so when only one parent is actively involved the child misses out. For instance, mothers are more likely than fathers to act as a child's social coach, helping them learn how to distinguish between appropriate and inappropriate behavior. Fathers more than mothers tend to play rough-and-tumble with their children. Children need both of their parents—let them have you."

- Blaine J. Fowers, Ph.D.
Blainefowers.com.
"Beyond the Myth of Marital Happiness: How Embracing the Virtues of Loyalty, Generosity, Justice, and Courage Can Strengthen Your Relationship,"
Used by permission

Everything Fowers says is what Cindy and I have been telling couples for years. It is exactly what we believe God is calling each and every one of us as individuals and as couples to live out every day. And each point is something we've experienced and employed in our marriage—and they work!

Something else I pray husbands come to understand (as I did) comes from the book Marriage Rebranded (pp. 71-72), written by Tyler Ward where he quotes something pastor Ray Ortlund told him:

"My wife was given to me to enrich me; to make me wiser, a better man, a better professional, and a better father... Once I stopped being so stubborn and learned to use our relationship and her voice as the asset that it is, everything changed."

In the subtitle of this last chapter we said, "Partner with God and with Each Other to Make an Impact on Your World." It is our prayer that this book has brought you to a place of realizing for the first time (or served as a refresher) that God has something much bigger planned for our marriages than what we can ever possibly imagine when we said, "I Do." He wants us to partner with Him in such a way that when people see our marriage, it would inspire them to want to know our God better.

We invite you to explore the www.marriagemissions.com website to see if there's anything else we can do to help you in your marriage. We cover over thirty different topics and have in excess of 1,500 free articles you can read/download for free.

The mission God gave us is very simple: **To Reveal and Reflect the Heart of Christ in Marriage**. We hope you will join us by adopting this as your mission as well.

We offer our prayer and our challenge to every person who has read this book:

> "May the God who gives endurance and encouragement give you a spirit of unity among yourselves as you follow Christ Jesus, so that with one heart and mouth you may glorify the God and Father of our Lord Jesus Christ!"
>
> - Romans 15:5-6
> NIV

> "May the Lord make you increase and abound in love for one another and for all, as we do for you, so that he may establish your hearts blameless in holiness before our God and Father, at the coming of our Lord Jesus with all his saints."
>
> 1 Thessalonians 3:12-13, NIV

> "...As you received Christ Jesus the Lord, so walk in him, rooted and built up in Him and established in the faith, just as you were taught, abounding in thanksgiving."
>
> - Colossians 2:6-7
> ESV

Your Personal Commitment

Now that you have read all The 7 ESSENTIALS to GROW YOUR MARRIAGE, it would be easy to just set them aside and think, Yeah, these are very practical tips that I/we should probably put into practice. But, if you're like us, our "best intentions" rarely get followed through on.

One thing Cindy and I learned a long time ago: if we put something in writing and post it in a conspicuous place to remind us, we are almost assured we will follow through on our commitment. Make two copies and both keep a copy in your Bible.

Therefore, below is each Essential stated as a commitment. Read them aloud together, pray for God to help you live them out every day, and then sign at the bottom indicating you are both committed to living these out.

WE DO COMMIT TO:

- I/We are committed, through God's help, to: BUILD AND MAINTAIN A SOLID FOUNDATION FOR OUR MARRIAGE – Committed to God and each other.

- I/We are committed through God's help to: BE INTENTIONAL IN GROWING OUR LOVE RELATIONSHIP.

- I/We are committed through God's help to: INVIGORATE OUR ROMANCE AND SEX LIFE WITH EACH OTHER.

- I/We are committed through God's help to: GUARD OUR HEART, MIND, AND MARRIAGE.

- I/We are committed through God's help to: FIGHT THE GOOD FIGHT: To resolve conflict in healthy ways.

- I/We are committed through God's help to: STAND UNITED: We won't let family, friends, or things separate us in our marriage.

- I/We are committed through God's help to: PARTNER WITH MY PARTNER: We will partner with God and with each other.

_____   _____

(Signed)   Signed

_____

(Date)

Marriage Missions International

Marriage Missions International got its name when God revealed first to Steve and then to Cindy, that every one of us become missionaries when we marry. It starts first with us, to continually live out the love of Christ in our own marriage, and then to reach out beyond to help others as well.

We knelt together to commit this ministry to God to take it where He would want it to go. It has been an awesome journey to help couples

REVEAL AND REFLECT THE HEART OF CHRIST WITHIN MARRIAGE.

If you would like to begin receiving our free weekly e-mail Marriage Insights, you can either go to their website at

www.marriagemissions.com

and click on SUBSCRIBE

Or you can send an e-mail to

subscribe@marriagemissions.com

and write "Subscribe" in the Subject Line.

Your information is never given or sold to any other entity.
We protect your privacy.

Made in the USA
Columbia, SC
26 October 2018